Understanding the Church Capital Campaign

By Michael Reeves

DISCIPLESHIP RESOURCES

P.O. BOX 340003 • NASHVILLE, TN 37203-0003

www.discipleshipresources.org

Cover and book design by Joey McNair

Edited by Debra D. Smith and David Whitworth

ISBN 0-88177-379-4

Library of Congress Control Number: 2002100806

DR379

Contents

Acknowledgments

There are many people who have helped me over the years in my understanding of the church capital campaign. First, thanks to those churches where I was allowed to serve as a staff member in the 1970's and 1980's. Their patience will forever be valued. I have also learned from the many churches I have been privileged to serve as a stewardship consultant. My understanding of the church capital campaign has grown with every campaign.

I also want to thank

• Sanford Coon, executive director of the New Mexico Conference Methodist Foundation, who contributed to Chapters 8 and 15.

• Ed Engleking, consultant with the Texas Methodist Foundation, for his contributions to Chapter 18.

• Jennifer Tyler, president of Tyler-Lokey and Associates from Irving, Texas, whose experience is reflected in her contributions to Chapters 3, 17, and 19.

• James Varner, vice-president of stewardship services for the Texas Methodist Foundation, whose experience with larger churches and major gifts is reflected in Chapter 9.

• Tom Locke, president of the Texas Methodist Foundation, who demonstrated an entrepreneurial spirit in establishing the stewardship department at the Foundation and hiring good people to staff it.

• The many professionals who taught me, including Charles Miller, founder of the Genesis Group; Ben Gill, chairman, and Bill Wilson, president, of Resource Services; Bob Cargill, founder of Cargill Associates; and Doug Laird and L. H. Coleman.

• My longtime friend Bob Ellis, of Garland, Texas, who prayed for me before, during, and after this project.

• Don Joiner and Herb Mather from the General Board of Discipleship of The United Methodist Church, who have contributed to my continued growth as a stewardship leader and specifically encouraged this project.

• The staff of the United Methodist Foundation of Louisiana, where I currently get to serve, who make a contribution to my life daily.

• My sons, Jason and Keith, who have been impatient for me to write this book for several years. And thanks to my wife, Mary, who had the patience for me to complete this project.

Foreword

Pastors and laity quake when they hear that a capital campaign is in the offing. They anticipate such an occasion in the same manner as they look forward to a root canal. In their unease they often fall into the practice of protecting pocketbooks rather than inviting generous gifts. The fear and mystique around major gifts is awesome.

The Hebrews felt that the name of God was so holy that one dare not utter the name. When they wrote about the deity, they used four consonants—*YHWH*. We put vowels between the Hebrew letters and came out with a word we could say—*Yahweh*. Modern Americans, on the other hand, seem to have no problem uttering the name of God. The unutterable holy word in churches in the twenty-first century is *money*. It is a wonder that we don't write it *MNY* in church publications.

Clergy have a double bind. They are supposed to be good at raising money but are not supposed to preach about it. No seminary teaches an aspiring pastor how to pull that off.

Committees on finance in most congregations look for every way they can to hold down expenses but spend little time in encouraging giving. They want to have more money to allocate but shrink away from asking for it.

Church leaders, of whatever ilk, tremble when they are faced with the need to raise "big bucks." Capital campaigns are outside the realm of training, familiarity, and comfort for most church leaders. When they hear about the costs of bringing in outside counsel to lead a campaign, they suddenly decide that it is pretty simple and "we can do it ourselves."

Unfortunately, they rarely come anywhere near their potential when they do it themselves.

This book is for those who need to know but may not even know what questions to ask. This book will take much of the mystery out of the mystique. It will not tell a committee how to do it, but it will tell them what they need to know in order to work well with those who have the knowledge and experience of leading capital campaigns.

Fortunately, there are people who are comfortable in inviting others to give. Many men and women invest their talents in directing capital campaigns. They have the gift to match people with a vision for ministry that requires generous giving—beyond the normal pattern. Dr. Michael Reeves is one of those people. He dares to describe the process in an open and nonthreatening manner without claiming that we should all be experts.

This book may not be "everything you wanted to know" about capital campaigns, but it surely is a good place to start. Michael Reeves provides us with a handbook to walk us through a process. He helps leaders in congregations work through many of the questions that a church faces when it recognizes the need to raise major funds beyond the normal budgetary needs. In fact, Michael provides needed answers to questions churches may not have known they should ask.

For about twelve years, our stewardship office at the General Board of Discipleship has looked for someone to write a book on capital campaigns. After several abortive attempts with other potential writers, we finally asked Dr. Michael Reeves to submit a proposal. He did exactly what we asked. Michael has provided a much-needed resource for leaders in congregations who have a vision for ministry but don't know how to take the big financial steps required to grow into the vision.

Now a word about what this book isn't. It is not a how-to-do-it manual for a committee to run its own campaign. If your church needs to raise any large sum of money you need outside counsel. You need counsel that "fits" with your congregation. *Extraordinary Money* will help you know the right questions to ask so that you can get the right fit.

This book will not relieve the leaders of a congregation from the task of making tough decisions. Readers will not find a magic formula about when to (or when not to) enter into a major capital campaign. However, Michael will help the leaders make a much more informed decision. The charts help you to compare your situation with that of other churches of similar sizes and similar goals for the funds.

Finally, I commend Dr. Reeves for relating fundraising to faith raising. If a campaign does not help people draw closer to God, no matter how much money is raised, it is not worth it. Why we do something must not be separated from how we do something. Even though Jesus seemed to constantly relate the use of one's money to one's relationship with the Holy One, we tend to separate the two. Michael reminds us over and over that the two cannot be separated if we are faithful to the gospel.

This is not a holy book. There are no magic formulas. However, it takes much of the puzzlement and mystification out of a process. I commend this book to you. It will help many congregations minister more effectively with the people of their community and the world. The process links the giver with his or her deepest faith values. Go. Raise extraordinary money for the glory of God! Celebrate the opportunity.

Herb Mather
Director, Center for Christian Stewardship
General Board of Discipleship
The United Methodist Church

Chapter One

For Such a Time as This

Introduction

Over the last few decades, hundreds of churches have faced the significant challenge of a building program. Sometimes this has been for new construction or renovation of existing facilities. Sometimes it has also included land acquisition, debt retirement, equipment needs, or a combination of all of these. Leader groups—including study committees, building committees, long-range-planning committees, and other creative titles—have considered the same problem: How are we going to pay for these capital needs? A church seldom has available funds for these projects, and although there can be significant agreement about the need, there are common concerns about the financial support. Inevitably, some think of borrowing the money for the project. Others think that the money can be raised from extra giving by the members. Many remember the stress of past building projects in churches they have attended and also have experienced or heard stories about fundraising attempts that fell woefully short of fulfilling the financial needs of the fundraisers. While some individuals might have confidence about how to proceed, there is often an anxious attitude among the leaders about what to do and how to do it.

It has been my observation that the church capital stewardship program has consistently generated more new revenue than any other single approach to funding. In my experience it is not uncommon for a church to receive two or three times the regular annual income in commitments over a three-year time period while enhancing the annual income base. Although personal discretionary income has exploded since the mid-1960's, the percentage of income regularly given to support the local church budget has continued to decline (see *The State of Church Giving Through 1998,* by John L. Ronsvalle and Sylvia Ronsvalle; Empty Tomb, Inc., 2000; pages 7 and 12). With the exception of the church capital campaign, the church has not done particularly well in stewardship initiatives in light of the growing prosperity of the culture. However, it is now common to find capital campaigns that range into the multimillion-dollar level. Smaller churches have raised substantial funds for building projects, and some larger churches have raised tens of millions of dollars for buildings, debts, missions, and endowments. Of course, there are also churches that have attempted a capital campaign and failed. Failure has included problems like not raising enough money, internal strife within the church family, ineffective communication, and many other variations that cause long negative memories that not only fail to build buildings but also fail to build the body of Christ.

Achieving Results

A successful campaign results in a broad base of financial support with substantial commitments made over a multiyear time frame designated toward the capital projects. At the same time, regular giving experiences additional growth. A successful campaign also brings about a sense of unity in the church family as they meet a common challenge and achieve a common goal. There is both an individual and a corporate experience that is positive and satisfying. This can be illustrated in the story of an individual family.

A few years ago a family attending a United Methodist church was asked to serve on the steering committee for a capital stewardship program. Their church had experienced significant growth and needed an educational building. The finance and building committee leaders wanted to raise as much as they could toward the cost of the new building to reduce the amount they would eventually borrow. When the couple agreed to serve they were told that they needed to do three things. They were asked to provide leadership on the steering committee, to complete some specific tasks in the campaign, and to pray about making the largest commitment they had ever made over and above their regular annual contributions. Their regular annual gifts were about $5,000. A few weeks into the campaign they were asked to confidentially share where they were in considering their capital campaign commitment. The wife indicated that they might contribute $5,000 over the three years and the husband said that they might be able to give as much as $12,000. They were challenged to continue to pray and remain open to the leadership of Holy Spirit. When the campaign progressed to the leadership challenge phase, the couple was invited to attend an advance-commitment dinner in a home. At the end of the evening the leaders were all challenged to consider making a significant commitment in advance of the rest of the congregation. They were instructed to take home a packet of information including a commitment card and to pray about their response. The couple listened, opened the packet, found the commitment card, filled it out, and brought it to the consultant as they were leaving. They said that they wanted the consultant to get the card to the church. When the consultant said that they were to take it home and pray about it one more time, they became upset. The husband said that they had prayed about this and could not afford to pray anymore. Their commitment had grown from estimates of $5,000 and $12,000 to $50,000. This family's experience of having their commitment grow has been repeated over and over as churches have conducted capital stewardship programs.

On the other hand, church leaders often assume that affluent families will automatically make large commitments. In one campaign, a wealthy church member known for substantial financial support for a church-related institution was encouraged to consider a $3 million commitment. After several weeks, and after encouragement from the senior minister as well as from affluent friends who had made similar large commitments, the individual made a modest commitment of a few thousand dollars. The ability and the awareness of the need were both present, but the motivation apparently was not.

These contrasting experiences raise a lot of questions:
- Why do capital campaigns work in some settings and not in others?
- What is the theological foundation in a capital campaign?
- How do church leaders build a consensus for an effective campaign?
- What kind of leaders are needed for a capital campaign?
- How does a capital campaign really work?
- What is a realistic expectation of how much can be raised?
- What is safe debt and how is it determined?
- What is the role of the pastor?

These questions and many more will be addressed in this book. The purpose is not to explain how to design and direct a capital campaign but rather to explain how to understand the dynamics that can contribute to an optimum result spiritually and financially.

Chapter Two

Fundraising or Stewardship?

The Theological Foundation

There is a distinct difference between an institutional fundraising campaign to obtain financial support for a needed building and a capital stewardship campaign in a local church. This distinction is often the difference between success and failure, between unity and disharmony, and between a modest response and a life-changing response. If a church is to have the optimum experience in a capital campaign, the difference between raising funds and realizing God's purpose must be established. The difference needs to be understood in the context of the theological foundation that establishes two goals.

A common misperception is that the goal of a capital campaign is the amount of money that the project will cost. Although seemingly logical, this false assumption is neither logical, accurate, nor spiritually based. When a committee works with an architect or builder, cost projections are based on square-footage costs, land costs, furnishings projections, and a variety of other factors. A common experience is that during construction the costs of materials vary, the costs of furnishings are revised, and change orders for modifications of the original construction plans generate additional costs. This is a normal part of the process in a construction project. There are also special circumstances that might arise, such as site-preparation problems, inconsistent delivery of construction materials, weather delays, and labor issues that could add costs after construction has begun. Finally, if the church begins the project using a construction loan, interim interest and loan costs add to the expense column. No matter what costs are projected, the real costs are not known until the construction project is completed. So to suggest that the goal of a campaign is the initial approximate cost from the architect or builder is to suggest a goal that is not accurate or even logical. The projected costs of the project and the related additions to costs identified present not the goal but rather the need.

Grounded in the Bible

Additionally, the spiritual goal is not related to an amount of money. The theological foundation that establishes the spiritual goal is a biblical basis found in both the Old and New Testaments.

Throughout the Bible, there are many verses that address financial matters. Some of these verses identify different kinds of giving. Tithing is a standard of giving taught in the Old Testament and mentioned several times in the New Testament. This was a regular giving to support the priesthood, religious celebrations, and benevolences. There is another kind of giving identified in the Old and New Testaments. This has to do with making commitments over and above regular tithes and offerings. One passage about this kind of giving is the story of the capital campaign in 1 Chronicles 29:1-9:

> King David said to the whole assembly, "My son Solomon, whom alone God has chosen, is young and inexperienced, and the work is great; for the temple will not be for mortals but for the LORD God. So I have provided for the house of my God, so far as I was able, the gold for the things of gold, the silver for the things of silver, and the bronze for the things of bronze, the iron for the things of iron, and wood for the things of wood, besides great quantities of onyx and stones for setting, antimony, colored stones, all sorts of precious stones, and marble in abundance. Moreover, in addition to all that I have provided for the holy house, I have a treasure of my own of gold and silver, and because of my devotion to the house of my God I give it to the house of my God: three thousand talents of gold, of the gold of Ophir, and seven thousand talents of refined silver, for overlaying the walls of the house, and for all the work to be done by artisans, gold for the things of gold and silver for the things of silver. Who then will offer willingly, consecrating themselves today to the LORD?"
>
> Then the leaders of ancestral houses made their freewill offerings, as did also the leaders of the tribes, the commanders of the thousands and of the hundreds, and the officers over the king's work. They gave for the service of the house of God five thousand talents and ten thou-

sand darics of gold, ten thousand talents of silver, eighteen thousand talents of bronze, and one hundred thousand talents of iron. Whoever had precious stones gave them to the treasury of the house of the LORD, into the care of Jehiel the Gershonite. Then the people rejoiced because these had given willingly, for with single mind they had offered freely to the LORD; King David also rejoiced greatly.

In this passage the spiritual goals and process begin to be identified. In the first verse the spiritual leader addresses the assembly and communicates that the project of building the Temple is for God, not for humans. The spiritual goal of seeing God's purpose accomplished and following God's leadership is obvious. In the next few verses David establishes that he gives regular offerings but is making a contribution in addition to his regular giving designated for the building of the Temple. The source of his gift is his own treasury or his accumulated wealth. His stated motivation is his devotion to the house of God. Then in the fifth verse, David asks who will accept his challenge, and thereafter the leaders make a substantial offering. Finally, the people joyously respond by giving freely with a single mind. This sequence shows a spiritual purpose for the campaign and leaders leading with commitments over and above regular giving, and the context is one of joyous response. There is no mention of a financial goal, a fair share, or implied guilt.

This story offers an illustration of resources being realized for a building. Other passages give additional spiritual principles. In 2 Corinthians 8:1-12, Paul attempts to motivate the leaders to fulfill a commitment they had made in a mission effort. Again, no financial goal is used, but encouragement to understand the spiritual principles involved is evident. In addressing the leaders of the church in Corinth, Paul sets a spiritual stage from the outset.

> We want you to know, brothers and sisters, about the grace of God that has been granted to the churches of Macedonia; for during a severe ordeal of affliction, their abundant joy and their extreme poverty have overflowed in a wealth of generosity on their part. For, as I can testify, they voluntarily gave according to their means, and even beyond their means, begging us earnestly for the privilege of sharing in this ministry to the saints—and this, not merely as we expected; they gave themselves first to the Lord and, by the will of God, to us, so that we might urge Titus that, as he had already made a beginning, so he should also complete this generous undertaking among you. Now as

you excel in everything—in faith, in speech, in knowledge, in utmost eagerness, and in our love for you—so we want you to excel also in this generous undertaking.

I do not say this as a command, but I am testing the genuineness of your love against the earnestness of others. For you know the generous act of our Lord Jesus Christ, that though he was rich, yet for your sakes he became poor, so that by his poverty you might become rich. And in this matter I am giving my advice: it is appropriate for you who began last year not only to do something but even to desire to do something—now finish doing it, so that your eagerness may be matched by completing it according to your means. For if the eagerness is there, the gift is acceptable according to what one has—not according to what one does not have.

Paul says that he wants to relate the grace of God given to sister churches. While specific cities are not identified, the church in Macedonia known for its generosity was the one Paul established at Philippi. Paul says that even though the churches had severe affliction and extreme poverty they still had joy and generosity. He says that they gave what they could afford and even more than they could afford and that they did it without any coercion. He admitted his surprise and then explained to the church leaders in Corinth why he thought the sister churches had such an attitude. He said they gave themselves first to the Lord and then to the leaders and the needs. Clearly, the motivation for generosity came first from a spiritual commitment. Paul praised the many good attributes of the Corinthian leaders but admonished them to not overlook this attribute of giving. Another critical issue in this passage is that the illustration Paul used was of churches that had limited financial resources. He told the leaders in Corinth that the issue was to respond with what they had, not with what they *didn't* have.

Goals

Based on these two passages, there seem to be two worthy goals in a capital campaign in a church. First, every family in the church should be informed and encouraged to prayerfully seek God's continuing will for them and their part in the church's mission and ministry. As a part of the body of Christ, when the body is moving in a specific direction, such as constructing a new building for expanding ministry, every family should determine its part in that direction.

The second goal is to raise as much money over and above regular giving as possible in order to minimize long-term debt and enable the church to continue to meet its operational and mission needs. Since the amount of money actually needed cannot be accurately determined before the completion of the project, a capital campaign affords the opportunity to raise as much money as possible, not only to address the capital needs but also to provide for unexpected needs related to the capital project and the expansion of ministry. One church established an early financial goal of $250,000 to build a new educational building. When the campaign resulted in more than $600,000 in commitments, they were able to expand their plans, pay all additional costs, and even have funds set aside to supplement budgetary support for the expanded ministries allowed by the building.

The nature of these goals also has implications for the design of the campaign. The relationship of the project to the mission of the church should be clearly communicated in the campaign, as David related the offering for the Temple to the purposes of God. The commitments are to be over and above regular giving. The leaders should set the pace, and the experience should be one of encouragement, not manipulation. These variables should be considered when the phases and activities of the campaign are planned. In the passage from 2 Corinthians, the motivation to give is a result of spiritual commitment, not of financial abundance. Again encouragement is a factor, and the issue of giving is seen as another spiritual expression in which the leaders in Corinth are encouraged to excel.

Asking the Right Questions

Often in a campaign, a church member will ask, "How do I know what to give if I don't know what the financial goal is?" Although sincere, it is the wrong question. The question suggested in the context of the passages considered is not what I can do for God but rather what God wants to do through me. Another question sometimes raised is "How do I know what I should give until I see the details of the plans for the project?" Agreement with the project is also not an issue in this theological context; the issue is God's continuing will. It is a spiritual issue, best determined in prayer. This core spiritual issue of God's continuing revelation individually and corporately is the dynamic difference between fundraising and a church capital stewardship approach. If individuals respond to God's leadership with a commitment that comes from a spiritual consideration, they are more likely to not only give but give with a confidence and generosity beyond mere fundraising. That is shown by the church in Philippi giving not just what they could afford but more than they could afford and then pleading for another opportunity to give even more.

One last theological consideration is the choice of words to be used in subsequent chapters. *Stewardship* is a word that has limited biblical basis, and refers to management, not fundraising. The application of the word *stewardship* to issues of financial giving is a recent development—the word *benevolences* was used through the late nineteenth and early twentieth centuries. Applying the word *stewardship* to financial giving is a result of recent church history and denominational program leadership. In the middle of the twentieth century the word *stewardship* became common in discussing financial giving to the church. It was about the same time that church-stewardship consulting companies began to emerge in the private sector. In the prosperity and population growth after World War II, churches began to grow and build in incredible numbers. As private firms developed and grew to help meet the need for extraordinary funds, the term *capital stewardship program* was used to suggest the difference between secular fundraising and the church's need for funds for ministry. Over the last fifty years, church culture has identified the process of raising money as a *church capital stewardship campaign,* a title that continues to have momentum in church life. For the purposes of this book, however, the term *capital campaign* will be used.

Chapter Three

Are We Ready?

The Preparation Phase

Many churches have an established process for developing both short- and long-term goals and objectives to help them pursue God's plan for the church in mission and ministry. Regardless of the process used, every church can benefit from the discovery of hidden problems or concerns within the congregational base. Some of these issues, if not addressed, could have a negative effect on ultimate funding decisions.

The initial precampaign discovery process, or precampaign survey, is sometimes referred to as a feasibility study. Yet the term *feasibility* often sends an uncertain message of "can we or can't we," "will we or won't we." First and foremost, embrace the fact that it is feasible for Christians to give to support the work of the church. Giving is an act of worship, an indicator of our spiritual depth. So, why send an uncertain signal at the beginning of the process that becomes fuel for a negative faction? *Precampaign planning* is a more positive term that conveys the idea of confidence. Before beginning, communicate the intent to leave no stone unturned in the effort to understand issues and hear concerns as well as to hear the hopes and dreams of the people.

In subsequent chapters, we will deal with the value and advisability of using professional counsel. Certainly the protocol for the survey process is most effective when done by someone not involved in the congregation. As an objective third party, a qualified, experienced professional can evaluate financial potential and state of readiness and interpret the input from the congregation in an unbiased manner.

Understanding the Environment Is Vital

Typically, when the church is anticipating raising funds above and beyond present tithes and offerings for special needs, three questions quickly surface in both "parking-lot" conversations and group discussions. The trilogy of inquiry includes: "Do we need it? Can we afford it? Is the timing right—are we ready?" These questions do not originate only from uninvolved persons. Frequently those involved in the planning process and church leaders ask the same questions. Failure to acknowledge and address these questions up front is a strategic mistake. Those who lead precampaign planning should be prepared to offer guidance to facilitate congregational discernment.

Addressing member concerns clears the path so the most important questions and answers can be heard: "What difference will the project make in the lives of people? What are the real ministry benefits? What will we be able to accomplish in ministry which we cannot achieve now?" The precampaign planning phase anticipates the questions and targets the issues.

Why not omit precampaign planning, cut to the chase, and let the people know it is time to give? It is a fact of human nature that people like to know their opinions are desired and valued. There is often suspicion among church members that important decisions are being made by a group commonly referred to as "they." No one really knows who makes up the "they" group, but the average person thinks the group does not include her or him. Precampaign planning validates that the congregation as a whole will be making important decisions about the future. Perhaps the best illustration of the importance of precampaign planning lies in a question: "If your people were asked to make gifts today toward the proposed project, would they make sacrificial commitments at the maximum level, or token contributions below their potential?" Here's the bottom line: people respond better when their opinions are sought prior to asking for a gift. This is one of the reasons that more money can be raised for new construction than for debt.

Every day, congregations meet and make decisions that will require extraordinary funding to carry out. Precampaign planning helps to market the appeal and to position the congregation to accept ownership for the proposed project. Simply because the church has agreed in principle to move forward does not mean the people have agreed in practice to accept their responsibility for giving to enable the project to happen. Making the decision is often the easiest part. Who among us has not purchased a new car or home, only to question the decision the next day? Buyer's remorse, or "price-tag shock," is real. It can become a deterrent unless addressed. Undertaking projects costing hundreds of thousands of dollars can be a scary proposition, even for people of faith.

Precampaign planning has a purpose and a destination. Often when congregations or institutions engage in seemingly endless discussion, constituents tune out. Excessive delays and procrastination are dynamic "deal killers." One strategic planning committee had been studying a proposal to relocate for ten years. The committee presented well-documented materials, catalogued in five three-ring binders. Page after page chronicled their trek of endless considerations, supported by every imaginable document. Those spearheading the planning process were extraordinarily capable engineers and planners in business. The study process became an ongoing program. Month after month the group met to discuss charts of projections. It was process without a destination. They were always "lathering" and never "shaving." They had gone as far as they could go. No priority or plan for closure had been set. They were boxed in, unable to proceed to the next level. Their pride of accomplishment gave way to weariness and fear, as year after year they saw the neighborhood and membership decline. The opposition to relocation was relieved that nothing ever came of the planning committee's work. Those who awaited direction lost hope.

Precampaign planning sets expectations for action. In one church a watercolor drawing of a proposed sanctuary was hanging in the church foyer. The discoloration on the matting indicated the artist's rendition was several years old. The pastor was asked about the drawing and explained that the picture was at least fifteen years old, as it had been hanging there long before he had arrived six years ago. At this point, the members no longer saw the drawing as a vision for the future but saw it only as artwork! Week after week, it was unnoticed by both members and visitors alike. A once vital plan for mission and ministry was now a reminder of unattainable dreams and unfulfilled plans. The congregation ought to have taken it down, put it away, and moved on toward newly inspired vision and renewed hope. Without expectations, the best visions sometimes become vague and relegated to the sidelines.

Precampaign planning engages people in thinking about the attainment of goals. As discussions about a project are initiated, expect the question "How can we hope to achieve these goals?" Without a projected plan to enable success, early discussions may be dismissed by members as frivolous thinking or a grand experience in "window shopping." When a plan for discernment and fundraising parallels early discussions, the congregation can begin to visualize success. A plan to achieve the goals gives members the permission to think big. Discovering attitudes and concerns and cultivating readiness are what precampaign planning is all about. Building consensus and ownership at the outset is critically important.

What Are the Objectives of Precampaign Planning?

In the preparation phase, precampaign planning should achieve the following:
1. Provide a welcoming, nonthreatening forum for member input.
2. Increase understanding of the mission needs motivating the project.
3. Cultivate major donors while discerning the state of readiness to participate, and thereby determine the best timing for the campaign.
4. Build consensus, interest, and enthusiasm and enhance momentum.
5. Identify possible campaign leaders.
6. Discover the financial potential that may be achieved.
7. Unearth concerns and issues that must be addressed in order to create the best possible climate for a successful capital campaign and for a positive congregational experience.
8. Establish a reference point for making important church decisions, a focal point for reporting back to the congregation, and a basis for refining the case statement and forming solid recommendations.

Where Should the Planning Process Begin?

The first step in defining and designing an appropriate process for precampaign planning is to clearly understand what has already occurred. Inquire about the types of planning and visioning activities the congregation has recently been engaged in and then objectively evaluate the results of these activities. Sometimes planning processes that appear to have congregational input are in fact primarily driven by staff or a committee. Cursory involvement of the congregation does not prepare people to give at maximum levels. People are rarely prepared to make sacrificial gifts toward a major capital project merely as a result of a committee report. The presentation of a master plan is not enough. Preparing for the campaign requires intentional commitment on the part of leaders to go the distance in mapping out a plan and seeking assistance where needed. Shortcuts can be costly and erode morale, trust, and interest.

Beginning with the case statement or list of objectives to be funded, precampaign planning involves the people in shaping and forming goals. It helps church leaders see the congregation and proposed project through the eyes of others.

Who Should Be Involved in a Precampaign Survey?

Every person in the congregation should be invited to be a part of the discovery and input process. Even those who choose not to participate will find value in being invited. You will want responses both from a broad base of constituents and from selected individuals representative of the congregation. There is a wide range of methods and procedures to use in the information-gathering process: communication packets mailed to homes, town-hall meetings, in-home gatherings, personal conversations, small-group forums, and more. All are vital aspects of building consensus. Those involved in making presentations about the project should be favorable toward it, knowledgeable of the details, prepared, and keenly aware of the mission needs that motivate the appeal. The essence of building consensus is involving the people, listening to their concerns, addressing the issues, and presenting the dynamic benefits of the project. Providing people a reason to want to give is the byproduct of building consensus.

Basic Elements and Tools for a Precampaign Survey

Basic elements in the precampaign survey should include
- a means for congregational input.
- a marketing plan to communicate the appeal.
- procedures for refining the objectives.
- tools for discovering financial potential.
- a plan of action to communicate how the funds can be raised.

Basic resources include
- a case statement or outline of mission objectives with associated cost estimates.
- a list of mission needs that will be realized as a result of the project.
- visuals, including drawings, master plans, and so forth.
- questionnaires for gathering congregational feedback.
- a schedule of gifts needed to achieve the projected goals.
- forums for discussion in both small- and large-group settings.
- a timeline for gathering, reviewing, and reporting information.

Be aware, however, that asking for congregational opinions and advice without responding can be a dangerous proposition. Safeguards are needed. For example, the protocol of the survey should include communication before, during, and after the process. Survey instruments should be designed from an objective viewpoint to draw out useful information that enables the attainment of the survey objectives.

What If We Discover We Are Not Ready?

If the precampaign process indicates that the congregation is not prepared for a successful campaign, then it should also identify the reasons for this. It should detail the steps to be taken to prepare the church, suggestions on how to address any unresolved issues that may exist, and procedures for measuring the effectiveness of interim plans. The precampaign phase culminates in a staff-committee focus group or retreat to discuss feedback received through the survey, including observations, recommendations, orientation about the capital campaign endeavor, and discussions of where to go from there.

Developing the Case Statement of Mission Objectives

The presentation of objectives to be funded should excite interest. The first basic case statement of objectives emerging from the long-range planning process is seldom "ready for prime time," though it is a vital resource document. Refinement is often needed to infuse the heart appeal and the inspiration motivating the vision. In a useful form, the set of objectives should communicate the details and inspire interest and the desire to participate.

Keep details simple. Avoid complicated, highly technical language that the average layperson might not understand or appreciate. Categorize the objectives in an appealing manner. Use language that connects the dollars with the fulfillment of the objectives. For example, if your project includes funds to renovate or build a sanctuary, consider referring to this as "Creating Space to Enhance Worship." There are many ways to present your objectives. Make the presentation appealing and creative. Plan to include the following components:

- Statement of the mission needs that inspire the planning process and objectives.
- Goals to be achieved (nonmonetary), including benefit to others.
- Objectives to be funded, in the most inspiring language possible and with the required dollars attached.
- Tasks or plan of action to achieve the objectives.

- Schedule of gifts needed to fund the objectives.
- List of various ways people can participate.
- Invitation to participate.

The Best Time for a Capital Campaign

The initial precampaign survey will determine the readiness of the people to support the capital campaign and the ultimate time frame most appropriate for launching the campaign. The best time will be determined by understanding when the highest attendance seasons are in the particular church. The final phases of the campaign should coincide with maximum church attendance times. Then the design can be developed in reverse. Generally, summer months are best used for formation and discovery types of activities.

Annual Campaign for Tithes and Offerings

The stewardship of giving requires intentional, continuing education. Most people agree that the church should do a better job of teaching stewardship. Generally, it is beneficial to the church to separate the capital campaign appeal from the annual budget campaign. This helps to emphasize personal growth in giving "above and beyond" one's usual pattern. Sometimes when the two appeals are combined, members are tempted to simply split an existing gift between capital and budget rather than take a step up in giving. Also, when churches commingle the two stewardship opportunities, neither receives its deserved focus.

Both the capital campaign and the annual campaign for tithes and offerings provide excellent opportunities for educating people about what the Bible has to say on giving. In the Bible we see two types of gifts: gifts that build the Temple, which come as additional offerings on unique occasions, and gifts that run the Temple, which are regular and ongoing. Great strides can be made in giving by simply defining what a tithe is. Use both stewardship opportunities to teach responsible financial stewardship to the fullest. By separating the two stewardship endeavors, churches make efforts to inspire and educate more effective. What appears to be the easiest approach is not always the best in achieving long-term goals for widening the base of stewardship. When correctly planned and scheduled, the two distinct campaigns maximize congregational involvement. When properly coordinated, the program formats consider proper use of staff and volunteer time.

Chapter Four

Building the Campaign Team

The Steering Committee

The next step in a capital campaign is the identification, enlistment, and training of a steering committee to lead the effort. There are a variety of philosophies about who ought to serve on this committee. Some suggest that an existing leadership group such as the building committee or the finance committee should serve as the steering committee for the campaign. Others think that the most affluent or generous should serve. However, as you think about the complexities of a capital stewardship campaign that will unfold over several months and affect the church's future ministry for several years, a special selected committee is the best option.

Characteristics of a Good Committee Member

While this chapter will present characteristics of individual positions on the steering committee, there are some general characteristics that are helpful in building a strong steering committee. The members should have the respect of the congregation as committed Christians with a positive attitude toward the church and the project. The capital campaign is a spiritual exercise with spiritual goals and needs the best possible spiritual leadership. This leadership should also have influence within the church, since involving others in the campaign is a significant part of most of the steering-committee positions. People who have demonstrated generosity both to the church and to the community beyond the church should be considered. The steering-committee members also ought to reflect the diversity within the church in terms of age, gender, ethnicity, length of membership, marital status, and personal financial ability. Finally, the steering-committee members need to model the process of praying about making a special financial commitment.

The design of the campaign and size and history of the church will determine specific positions needed and the number of people required in each position, but there are some common tasks and qualifications that can be used to identify steering-committee members.

Campaign Director

Every campaign needs to have a leader for the steering committee. The leader should be one of the most respected and influential people in the congregation. Sometimes using more than one campaign director can address different spheres of influence or church leadership. The campaign director should be the primary spokesperson for the campaign. Usually the campaign director will preside at steering-committee meetings, monitor campaign activities, attend major campaign meetings, and lend his or her credibility to the campaign.

The campaign director is also often asked to be a part of the leadership-gift or major-gift team. One of the reasons is the sensitivity and importance of the leadership-gift phase of the campaign, and another is that the campaign director is often one of the most substantial potential donors. In one church, two campaign directors were used who together exemplified almost all of these characteristics. One was a highly respected older member who had more limited financial ability but was recognized in the church and the community as a patriarch. Since he was retired, he had more time to give to the campaign, and he brought substantial credibility to the effort. He also related to the senior adults in the church who were more conservative. The other campaign director was a young professional who had less time but more financial capacity and was respected as a current and future leader by the younger and middle-aged adults in the congregation. Working together, they provided excellent leadership that was stronger than either could have brought by himself.

Administrative Coordinator

This position is sometimes called campaign secretary or administrative assistant. This position is so critically important to the smooth working of the campaign that it is referred to as the "nerve center" of the campaign. Usually this person has executive secretarial skills, but a wide variety of people have served effectively in this role. Retired military personnel, retired teachers, a surgical nurse on a leave of absence, and retired administrative personnel have all filled this role well. This position is one of the two positions that require the most commitment of time.

Existing church secretaries are sometimes considered for this position, but that is seldom a good idea. There is a significant amount of work to be done, and the best approach is for an administrative coordinator with a single focus on campaign priorities to work with the church administrative staff.

This position is responsible for the overall administrative support of the campaign, including scheduling and arranging room assignments for all meetings, preparing materials for meetings, attending a majority of meetings, monitoring the enlistment process, coordinating all mailings in the campaign in cooperation with the church office, reminding people of meetings during the campaign, and serving as the central point of all communication between the steering committee, church members, staff, and consultants. Often a steering-committee member or a church member will want to discuss things with the consultant, such as details of an assignment or matters concerning their personal financial commitment. The administrative coordinator is the conduit for setting those meetings in most cases. There might also be some assistants for this position, depending on the size of the church and the personality and skills of the person serving.

Communication Director

This position can also be called publicity director or promotional director. This is the other position that will require the most time in the campaign. The communication director coordinates all of the campaign's publicity and promotional materials. Every campaign will have its own materials, and they may include a fact sheet, a brochure, prayer support pieces, visual aids, campaign newsletters, information booths, commitment cards, invitations to special events, a letterhead, a logo design, campaign titles, video presentations, and bulletin inserts. The person serving in this position should have an aptitude for the tasks that could be seen in a background of public relations, journalism, writing skills, advertising, marketing, or some field of communication. But the specific tasks are secondary to the ability to manage a production schedule. Assistants with specific skills in technical areas can be enlisted or hired, but campaign deadlines must be met for the communication efforts to have optimum impact. This person must be able to work cooperatively with the administrative coordinator as well as the church staff, campaign director, and consultant.

Home-Visitation Director

A common activity in a campaign is to build an organization to visit every home and deliver some information about the campaign. This serves to confirm membership and update addresses as well as provide hand delivery of important information. The desired outcome of home visitation is to have the membership informed and in prayer about the campaign; but this is not a canvassing visit where commitment cards are provided. This is an informational contact.

Some campaigns might have home gatherings supplemented by direct mail and calling to accomplish the same task, but the characteristics for the position are the same. There will often be several home-visitation directors who work together to build the visiting organization.

The overall organization needs to provide one visitor or visiting unit for every six to eight families in the congregation. A home-visitation director usually enlists several assistants who are trained and then enlist another level of participants. In larger churches, an additional level is some-times used to have enough visitors to complete the task. The director must monitor the subsequent enlistments and help where needed. This person should be someone who is outgoing, positive, and encouraging to others.

Prayer-Support Director

The prayer-support director is someone who promotes prayer for the campaign throughout the process in ways that are consistent with the spiritual experiences, practices, and culture of the church. The capital campaign is a spiritual journey, and praying for enlistment, involvement, statements of support, effective communication, substantial commit-ments, and a positive spirit supports the entire campaign. People who have demonstrated mature spiritual leadership or who might have been involved in existing prayer ministries serve well in this role. Existing prayer ministries can also be used in this campaign.

Leader-Commitment Director

This position has also been called advance-commitment director, major-gifts director, or special-gifts director. In a capital campaign, leadership gifts are necessary to set a pace, to establish credibility, and to achieve a maximum financial result. This person will work closely with the senior minister, the campaign director, the administrative coordinator, and the consultant to identify, solicit, and receive commit-ments from leaders in the congregation. This is a delicate and critically important task. The leader of this task needs to help develop a list of potential leaders, establish some home fellowships for the challenge, and enlist some assistants to help. This person should also have influence with those who have the largest financial potential and should be exemplary in her or his own commitment.

Major-Event Director

In almost every campaign some kind of general church gathering or assembly is used as a climactic event in the campaign. This is where the church that might have several worship services gets together at one time in one place. The major-event director manages the logistical details of the event. Details include where and when to meet to assure maximum participation, food, children's activities, entertainment needs prior to the program, and management of related costs. While another organization will receive reservations and communications will provide invitations, all other details fall to the major-event director. This is not a covered-dish dinner but, usually, a catered event requiring a lot of detail coordination. People who have put together trade shows, worked conventions, or coordinated similar events should be considered for this role.

Hospitality Director

This position supports the major event by building an organization to call all of the church members and receive their reservations as well as assist in a variety of ways at the major event. Like the home-visitation director, the hospitality director will enlist assistants who enlist others. While the task is simple and does not require very much time, it is an effective way to involve a lot of people who might have had limited church participation.

Commitment Director

This position used to be called canvass director or solicitation director, but those titles and the methods associated with them are seldom used anymore. This person builds a small organization of people to follow up commitment day with either calls or written notes to those members who have not yet responded. The task has become one of information and encouragement instead of the old model of canvassing the homes. The best person for this job is a person in sales because of the perseverance such people usually have.

Other Positions

There are many other possible steering-committee positions that might be used depending on campaign design and the individual church.

Age-group coordinators for children, youth, college-age people, singles, and senior adults might be needed in some churches. Sometimes a church has a history of receiving memorial and tribute gifts, and that would also require a steering-committee leader. These optional positions should only be used when necessary to address specific needs within the church.

Identifying the individuals to serve in these responsibilities is usually the role of the senior minister with counsel from trusted staff and laypeople.

Enlisting the Steering Committee

In most churches, the pastor will enlist the steering committee. This enlistment needs to be an intentional scheduled event with the pastor following a consistent, established approach. Follow these general guidelines:

- For each steering-committee position, prepare a list of people who could fill the role well. Determine how many of each type of director you will need (How many home-visitation directors? How many commitment directors? and so forth). Also remember that a person may qualify for more than one position.
- Establish the enlistment schedule by ordering positions and people. Start with the campaign director and work down to less critical roles. Remember that if someone is a likely "second choice" for a key position, you should not discuss alternative positions with her or him until that key position has been filled. (In one church a potential campaign director had some reasons that campaign director would not be the best role to accept. There was another position that worked better for this person, and a different campaign director was selected.)
- The steering-committee list should be reviewed with the professional consultant before the people on the list are actually contacted. This can be done by phone and will assist the pastor in reviewing the process and people one final time.
- For those positions requiring more than one leader, like home-visitation director, it is best to meet with each person or couple individually. If the steering committee is large, however, it may become necessary to use one appointment to see several people who are filling the same specific position.
- Most enlistment interviews require thirty to forty-five minutes. The meetings can take place at church or at the person's work or home and should begin on time.

- The pastor should call to set up the appointments if possible, and no more information should be shared than necessary to secure the appointment. The most common way to explain the purpose of the visit is to say, "I have an idea of how you might be able to assist the church and me in our capital campaign, and I would like to discuss it with you." If more than a couple of days pass between the request for the appointment and the meeting itself, a reminder call should be made.

- In the enlistment interview, the pastor should give a summary of the project and a general explanation of the campaign and then describe what he or she is asking the person to consider doing in the campaign. One way of verbalizing this is "I need your help. After prayerful consideration, I would like you to think about serving as a leader in our capital campaign." Then, using the campaign calendar and the job description for the position, you can describe the responsibilities. A good way to conclude the enlistment is to summarize like this: "You are being asked to do three things: first, to lend your credibility and leadership to the steering committee; second, to serve in this specific task; and third, to be willing to pray about making the largest financial commitment you have ever made." Give the person the opportunity to say yes in the interview. If more time is needed, set a specific date and time for a response.

- When a person accepts a position, tell him or her the training time for the steering committee. Follow up the verbal information with a letter of appreciation and confirmation about the time of the training.

Look for ways to express your appreciation for the service of those who become leaders and for ways to encourage them in their responsibilities.

This enlistment process will also model effective enlistment procedures for the steering-committee members who must enlist assistants as a part of their responsibilities. The administrative coordinator and the communication director should be alerted to the commitment of time needed in their individual assignments. No one should be told that the job is easy or will not take much effort for the sake of getting a yes. Spending the time and energy to do the enlistment of the steering committee is one of the most important things the pastor will do to assure the success of the campaign. Most problems in capital campaigns can be averted if an effective steering committee is enlisted properly.

Training the Steering Committee

The training of the steering committee has already begun if they are enlisted as described in the preceding section. Generally, the training will be done by a professional consultant and will include several topics. The steering committee needs to understand the spiritual foundation of the effort in order to distinguish this from other secular efforts they might have known. They also need to have a good understanding of the project, including not only what is being done but also how it relates to and enhances the ministry objectives of the church. Then the steering committee needs to understand the flow of the campaign by reviewing the calendar and the supportive materials. Their specific responsibility should be clearly identified, and the relationships between tasks should be explained. Committee members should receive guidelines for effective enlistment of assistants along with an offer of help from the pastor and campaign director. Then the conclusion of the training should focus on the personal prayer and personal financial commitment needed for a successful campaign. The desired outcome of the training is for the steering-committee members to have a general understanding of the importance of the campaign and their role in it. The process of training—which began with the pastoral enlistment, continued in specific training, and was supplemented with training materials—will continue with a steering-committee review within a couple of weeks of the training and with individual meetings to review specific dates for completion of tasks.

Chapter Five

Equipping the Saints

Role of the Senior Pastor and Staff

When a church is in a capital campaign the regular and seasonal activities of the church do not diminish. Sometimes it feels as if all of these things actually increase. It is important that the senior pastor and staff know what their responsibilities are related to the campaign. In Ephesians 4:11-12, Paul suggests that the purpose of the pastor is "to equip the saints for the work of ministry, for building up the body of Christ." The capital campaign offers a model of how the pastor, staff, and steering committee work together as a cohesive team with everyone having an important role in implementing the plan.

One of the greatest concerns and the most often asked question concerning the pastor's role is whether or not he or she will be expected to personally ask for financial commitments. The answer is not simple. While many pastors do not want to know about individual levels of contribution and others are specifically denied access to that information, the pastor needs to work with the leadership-commitment organization in the campaign. If giving is considered a spiritual decision, it seems logical that the pastor would have a role. The nature of this role has to be explored in the context of the church environment, the campaign design, and the pastor's ability. One approach that has proven helpful to most pastors is to have a list of the top twenty-five to fifty donor families in the order of giving to use in the selection of the steering committee. It is not unusual for the list to yield names not already identified as potential leaders. In some churches, pastors have expressed that they did not know some of the families on the list, and their opinion of the value of that knowledge has changed. In those campaigns that have the greatest financial success, the pastor is often directly involved in the cultivation of the leading gifts.

Financial Commitment

Another major responsibility of the senior pastor is setting an example with her or his own financial commitment. The pastor is seldom expected to be able to provide one of the lead gifts, but when pastors have made pacesetting gifts and shared their level of commitment with the steering committee, the steering committee has often been challenged to grow in their own financial commitments. Consultants relate that one of their most disappointing experiences is the conversation with the senior pastor when there is an inability or a lack of willingness to reveal a personal financial commitment. In some campaigns, the consultants have to request that the pastor not share the commitment because it would have an adverse effect on the steering committee. On the other hand, the positive and significant financial commitment of the senior pastor has been one of the most influential ingredients in many campaigns. In one church a senior pastor who had planned to retire about three years after the campaign shared his commitment with the steering committee. The steering committee members knew that this would be the minister's last big project before retirement and had not expected a commitment at all, much less a commitment that reflected a real priority. The impact raised the level of commitment for the whole committee. The senior pastor's financial commitment needs to be established early in the campaign.

Other Responsibilities

In addition to identifying and enlisting the steering committee, assisting in the leadership-commitment organization, and making a personal financial commitment, here are some other responsibilities of the senior pastor:

The pastor's and church's calendars must reflect a priority for the campaign. While this might seem logical, it seems to be a common problem in calendar considerations that some business-as-usual activities take priority over campaign activities. This ought to be discussed and decided in the planning phase before meeting dates and times for the campaign are set. When a major training meeting or leadership-commitment event is planned, other church activities that would conflict should not be added to the schedule. When the pastor decides to lead a trip to the

Holy Land in the midst of an intense phase of the campaign, it sends a clear message of what the church's priorities really are. The capital campaign cannot be relegated to a less significant role than other church activities.

The pastor needs to attend all steering-committee meetings, all major training meetings, and other meetings upon request. The professional consultant will help the pastor identify which meetings are particularly important.

The communication director will need the senior pastor's counsel concerning printed materials, including advice on the selection of the title and logo for the campaign.

With the pastor's steering-committee enlistment completed, most of the steering committee will be asking others to join them to help in their respective tasks. The pastor can help by publicly encouraging the involvement of church members and privately recommending assistants.

When the campaign begins to intensify, the senior pastor should work with the campaign director to identify and enlist individuals to give statements of support. These statements, shared in worship, small groups, and written materials, are extremely important and should reflect the various constituencies within the church.

Finally, the senior minister needs to preach throughout the campaign addressing those subjects which will help or challenge the particular congregation. Issues of prayer, commitment, and priorities are helpful at any time in the campaign. In the intensive phase, sermons should be highly motivational and clear in their focus. It seldom helps a campaign for the senior minister to adhere to a preaching plan that does not relate to or acknowledge the capital campaign. The professional consultant will usually have helpful resources.

Leaders in multiple-staff churches should give attention to the role all staff will have in the capital campaign. The senior minister should relate to all steering-committee members as needed. However, in larger churches with larger steering committees, other staff may be assigned to offer encouragement, pray, and assist specific steering-committee members. This serves to affirm the steering committee and involve the staff. A timely call, written note, or cup of coffee can make a big difference to church members who have agreed to serve in a leadership role. All staff should be encouraged to prayerfully consider their financial commitment.

There are many things the senior pastor and staff can do to contribute to the success of the campaign. There are also things that they can do that will damage the campaign. Two weeks after one senior pastor shared a particularly modest three-year financial commitment with great emotion, he bought a very expensive vehicle. The pastor's priorities were demonstrated very clearly. When the preaching plan does not include topics relevant to the campaign, congregations are less likely to see the campaign as a spiritual matter. When the pastor adds distractions, either through additional church activities or through personal absences at critical points in the campaign, the campaign will suffer. And when the pastor privately communicates less than wholehearted support for the projects or the campaign, the impact is public. Sometimes it seems that there is a lack of common sense during a capital campaign.

Chapter Six

Building
Ownership

Organizational Development

There are two things that make a campaign achieve maximum spiritual and financial results. One is the level of individual gifts, and the other is broad-based participation in the campaign. In our culture there is a strong push for us to be spectators instead of participants. This is seen in the language used in casual conversations. Many church participants speak in terms of "they," referring to leadership, staff, and others in their church. Their perspective is that what is happening at the church is being led and directed by others. This is not always a negative view about what "they" are doing, it is just a way of expressing that until what is expected and asked of the speaker is clear, the process belongs to others. It might also result from lack of knowledge. In church life today we can no longer assume an informed constituency. It doesn't matter that we have written, called, mailed, visited, and had meetings about the direction. It doesn't matter how well-thought-out the plans are or how logical or obvious the need is. Members in our churches are asked to process enormous amounts of information, and until information is presented as something that affects their lives and calls for some sort of response, they are likely to remain spectators. Obviously a good communication plan needs to be developed with materials that communicate in different ways. However, one of the first and strongest ways to broaden the base of participation is to involve people in the campaign activities. When more people are involved and given some ownership of the campaign, there is a higher response in the financial commitments ultimately received.

It might seem that when a project is clearly needed, presented, discussed, and approved, involving people in accomplishing the project would not be too large a challenge. However, in church life we have often asked people to serve and promised them that not much would be required. Later they found that the job was much more demanding and required a longer and more significant commitment than originally expected. This causes some people to be hesitant to make any commitment of their time. In addition, many people have a fear of having to ask others for money or being asked themselves. Although they might be in favor of the plans and the campaign, the idea of their direct involvement in solicitation and their personal commitment of time are distasteful at best. We live in a culture where people want eternal credit for minimal cost, and this attitude can adversely affect a capital campaign unless handled effectively.

In a well-designed capital campaign, the steering-committee members are the leaders who involve others most effectively. Some steering-committee positions will need more assistants than other positions. The communication director, major-event director, and the administrative coordinator may need to enlist some help based on specific skills needed for the task. The number of people and required skills will vary, but intentional enlistment is still necessary. However, the home-visitation director, hospitality director, leader-commitment director, and commitment director need to develop large organizations to complete their tasks. A proven way to involve people and build larger organizations is to use what is called pyramidal enlistment. It is based on the idea that everyone has a circle of influence, knowledge, and relationships within the church. It might relate to a small group in which they participate or it might be long-established friendships. The way pyramidal enlistment works is that the director enlists several assistants. The assistants are trained and asked to enlist another level of workers. In some larger churches, the third level is trained and asked to enlist a final level of workers. That means that one director can enlist five assistants; five assistants can enlist four captains each; and each of the captains can enlist two additional team members. Ideally, that would result in sixty-five people for every director. Using this method no one has to enlist more than five people. Of course, the weakness of the pyramidal system lies in the standard of enlistment and the assumption that people will attend the training and get all the facts concerning the task. If three levels of enlistment can be used instead of adding the fourth, it works more effectively.

Effective Enlistment Approaches

Pray about the enlistments. One feature of steering-committee enlistment is the pastor saying, "After prayerful consideration, I would like you to think about serving...." The same approach should be carried to every level of enlistment.

Enlist personally. The best way to enlist someone is face-to-face. When a limited number of people need to be enlisted by any individual and there are two to four weeks to enlist them, a face-to-face meeting should be attempted first. This allows a focused interaction where the one enlisting can explain the campaign, outline the task, and give a written job description that includes training dates and dates for the task to be accomplished. There is great value in looking someone in the eye and saying, "I need your help."

Present the job description. It is helpful to explain the nature of the specific organization and the task and encourage a positive feeling about the campaign. Describe the purpose of the team and invite discussion to answer questions the person might have. This explanation of what the job at hand is, when the training is, when the task will be performed, and when the task will be completed should be clear and concise.

Offer support. It is important for the person being enlisted to know that he or she is a part of a team, that training will be provided, and that others will be helping to accomplish the task. Expressing confidence in the person's abilities, giving assurance of adequate preparation, and emphasizing the support of the leadership will help the enlistment.

Close the deal. The person should be given the opportunity to accept the responsibility at the end of the conversation. If the person needs more time, establish a short deadline for the response. After someone has said yes, a written note or personal call should follow in a couple of days affirming their acceptance, repeating the training date and time, and expressing thanks. The name needs to be reported to the administrative coordinator so the person can be reminded of the training session again.

Sometimes when initially asked, people will decline to serve. They might not have been receptive for some reason or they might not want to participate at the level being asked. Some people will participate in the task if they do not have to enlist others. Save those names to pass on at the next level of enlistment.

Approaches to Avoid

Do not rely on the pastor's announcement from the pulpit encouraging people to serve. This might set a climate of acceptance but people still need to be personally asked about a specific job.

Do not make a general announcement for help and expect a response. The people who respond to a general announcement might or might not do what is needed. The explanation of the job with the specific information about training and task is very important.

Be careful about enlisting by phone. A common phone response is "I'll try to help" or "If you can't get enough people to help, give me a call." If those are counted as positive responses, the organizational development will suffer. When reminded of a training session, a phone respondent might well say, "I just said that I might help." This indecisive method can create a negative spirit about the campaign.

Try to not "catch" or "trap" people between church activities at the church and enlist them. Enlistment merits focused time.

Don't tell people that what they are being asked to do is easy or will require very little time. Some of the responsibilities are easy and require minimal time, but the message that the person needs to hear is that he or she is being asked to do something in the campaign that is important and will contribute to the success of the campaign.

In most campaigns the administrative coordinator will remind the newly enlisted person of the date, time, and location of the training. In order to do this, the coordinator needs to know who has been enlisted. The administrative coordinator's job is complicated when the names are not reported in a timely fashion. Then he or she will be forced to make calls to the one doing the enlisting to identify who else needs to be called. Sometimes it is helpful for the administrative coordinator to have an assistant whose sole responsibility is to monitor the enlistment process.

While all of this enlistment detail can feel overwhelming, it is one of the many differences often found between a professionally-led effort and a self-led effort. This level of detail results in accountability and a broadening of the base of participation. Many leaders assume that others share their understanding and enthusiasm even though they have not been involved. Involving others is critical to a successful campaign.

Chapter Seven

Including the Holy Spirit

The Spiritual Foundation

We believe that God's will for individuals as well as communities of faith continues to be revealed. Different denominations view the manifestation of God's will in different ways, but there is general agreement that understanding God's will is a continuing process in a pilgrimage of faith. This is also true in giving. In 2 Corinthians 8:5 Paul explains that the spirit of generosity seen in the churches in Macedonia was a result of their commitment to the Lord and their understanding of God's will. The first goal of the capital campaign is to have every family of the church informed and in prayer about God's will for them with regard to the campaign. It is not uncommon after a capital campaign for church members to talk more about the spiritual experience than the amount raised.

The Role of Prayer

One of the ways that Christians discern God's will for their lives is through prayer. Since responding to God's will is a primary goal of the campaign, encouraging individuals to pray and creating opportunities for prayer are key components in a successful campaign. Some churches have relied on the prayer-support directors to use existing prayer ministries or to create new opportunities to enhance the prayer life of members during a campaign. Since the capital campaign is related to the ministry goals of the church, prayer is appropriate and important. While people might have a variety of views on the value and practicality of prayer as related to a church capital campaign, there are many experiences of extraordinary giving, changes in attitude, and enhancement of projects that can be attributed to the power of prayer during a campaign.

The Importance of Small Groups

Faith is nurtured through the many small groups found in congregations. It is through Sunday school classes, Bible study groups, Covenant Discipleship groups, and so forth that members have the opportunity to engage in spiritual conversation with other Christians seeking to grow in faith. However, due to its more intimate nature, the small-group setting can also be a place where negative attitudes are expressed. There is seldom an intentional effort to be negative, but uncertainty and lack of accurate information blended with any previous negative experience raising funds make less-than-positive attitudes flourish.

It is helpful if leaders of small groups are well informed about the ministry objectives of the campaign. These leaders can be an important source of support for the campaign and can help members of the small groups they lead understand the campaign's theological and spiritual basis. Small groups can be encouraged to study topics or Bible passages that relate to the purposes of the campaign and the ministry objectives of the church. Small groups have enormous influence in a community of faith, and churches need to intentionally engage them during the campaign without co-opting their primary purposes.

The Value of Testimonies

Testimonies or statements of support can be extremely helpful in encouraging people and raising the vision and level of giving. There are a lot of opinions about how and when to present testimonies, and there are situations where the wrong kind of statement of support can have a negative impact—for example, when the pastor reveals a particularly modest personal commitment or uses the opportunity to complain about low pay or personal financial challenges.

On the other hand, an influential testimony can be presented by an individual with modest resources. One controversy in this area is whether people should publicly disclose the specific amount of money being committed. Some believe that making public the largest commitments will encourage the rest of the members. Others believe that it is spiritually inappropriate to ever disclose specific dollar amounts. As in many church disagreements, the truth lies somewhere in the middle. Forcing individuals to give financial testimonies can backfire if people feel that others are critical of the amount they are giving. Some people have found that after they disclosed how much they were giving in a requested testimony, some of their relationships within the church changed. Asking people to disclose publically the specific amount they are giving also encourages expressions of pride that are inappropriate. However, in 1 Chronicles 29 David did make a public commitment, and the total cumulative amount given by other leaders is described. In biblical times, giving was done publicly and not through a secret envelope system.

The following guidelines for testimonies are helpful. It is good to cultivate statements of support from individuals who represent the demographics of the congregation. The statements can be presented in verbal presentations in small groups and public worship and they can also be presented in written form in newsletter and bulletin inserts. The purpose is to build credibility and encourage others to participate. One approach that helps is to provide some written guidelines and then have a group meeting with the people who are being asked to share their commitments. At this meeting they can talk through the testimony they plan to give. It is also helpful if the pastor, a staff member, or the campaign director is available to meet individually with those who are giving verbal statements to let them rehearse. It is helpful to write out verbal testimonies to avoid rambling and stage fright.

A starting point for developing a meaningful statement of support is answering these questions in three to five minutes:

- What is your name?
- Who is your family?
- Where do you work?
- How long you have been a member of or participant in the church?
- How do you see God leading in the church?
- Why will you participate financially?
- How are you and your family trying to make the decision of how much to commit to the campaign?
- What is the significance of your financial commitment? Is it causing you to give something up or change something you do?

Those giving testimonies should conclude by inviting others to join with them and invest in the future of the church.

Scriptural Foundation

In addition to statements of support, small-group involvement, and prayer activities, relevant sermons and lessons can also help establish the spiritual foundation for a capital campaign. From the 1950's through the mid-1970's, a common text preached and taught during building campaigns was Nehemiah 2–7. While that text about building the walls is a good biblical story, it is certainly not the only one that can be used. Here are a few ideas:

Exodus 3–4 tells the story of Moses' reluctance to participate in God's plan for him. He gave several reasons why he could not do what was being asked, and God answered each reason. This could be used early in the campaign when people are being asked to become involved.

Numbers 13–14 is the story of the spies sent by Moses to spy out the land of Canaan. While all the spies agreed that the project of claiming the land was good, ten of the twelve focused on the challenges they thought were overwhelming. They led the people to fear instead of faith, and the leaders agonized about the response. Only Caleb and Joshua exhibited faith to go forward. This would be an excellent passage to address attitude, meeting a challenge, the impact of negativity, and the agony of leadership.

First Chronicles 29 offers the story about David raising the resources for the Temple to be built. It could be used as a sermon or lesson for small groups and can also be used as a resource for training meetings in the campaign.

Second Corinthians 8-9 is the encouragement Paul gave to the leaders in the church at Corinth about a special mission offering to support the saints in Jerusalem. This text addresses giving from limited resources and of course underscores priorities and discovering God's will. This could also be good teaching or preaching material.

Paul's letter to the church at Philippi is in part a response to a generous heartfelt gift. There are applicable passages throughout the letter, like Philippians 4:4-6 about peace of mind, 4:8 about godly attitudes, and 4:13 about spiritual confidence in the face of challenges.

Chapter Eight

Telling the Story

Campaign Communications

Some people assume that raising funds for a church building project consists of a sermon or two, a couple of well-worded letters, and some really good pulpit announcements. This approach has ended a great deal of momentum in the lives of many churches. We make a poor judgment when we assume that we have an informed constituency in most of our churches. We also hurt our efforts when we believe that people will read everything that is mailed to them or listen to all the verbal presentations that are made. The key to effective campaign communication is to tell the story in as many ways as we can imagine as many times as we can, repeating a simple story—God's continuing direction for the church. For many years, the primary communication piece was a slick, brightly colored brochure that followed a prescribed outline and design. In today's culture, however, we need to develop a comprehensive communication package targeting the person who attends the church once a month. If we can get the message to that person, then most who will respond will have the necessary information.

An effective communications team will have a director who can manage the process and meet deadlines. The team could include someone who can coordinate the printing of brochures or other print pieces, a photographer, a graphic artist, a copywriter, an information-booth coordinator, and people with other technical skills needed to carry out your communications plan. The administrative coordinator will need to work closely with this team. Additionally, the pastor and campaign director need to be continually informed of the plans and actions of the communications team.

Getting Started

The first decision that needs to be made is what the title or theme of the campaign will be. A theme that used to be used frequently was "Not Equal Gifts but Equal Sacrifice." This theme can still work in some settings. However, the word *sacrifice* does not resonate in our contemporary culture as strongly as it once did. Many other themes have been used effectively, and the right title or theme should be discussed with the pastor and campaign director. The artistic expression of the title (the logo) should be presented to the steering committee at their first training session or at least by their first check-up meeting. Often a biblical theme will emerge or a title will come from some aspect of the church's project or history.

Once the title for the campaign has been settled, the next step should be the development of a fact sheet. One way to develop a fact sheet is to create an interview situation with the pastor, campaign director, building-committee chair, and the architect. Scheduling such a meeting can be a challenge, but it has lasting value in the campaign. The communication director can ask basic questions about both the project and the campaign and draft a fact sheet in an interactive style of questions with concise answers. Typical questions are:

- What is the project?
- Why are we doing this project?
- When are we planning to build?
- Who will benefit most from the building?
- How much will it cost?
- Why are we having a capital campaign?
- What are the title and theme of the campaign?
- Who is leading the campaign?
- What are the major campaign dates?
- What kind of commitment will I be asked to make?

The fact sheet should answer who, what, why, when, where, and how about two subjects—the building plans and the capital campaign. Another value of this process is the clarification of answers. One thing that delays the production of printed pieces is uncertainty about the right answers. With the participants identified, questions can lead to clarified or agreed-upon answers. This process also offers the opportunity for some video or audio production if that is a part of the communications plan.

The fact sheet is often used as a part of home visitation and the call to prayer.

Visual Support

Supporting visual materials need to be developed for use in the promotion of prayer as well as throughout the campaign. The prayer-support director might want to develop some targeted prayer materials such as a prayer calendar, printed prayers, or a devotional guide. Producing such material is the responsibility of the communications team. There is no need for a separate spiritual theme or logo for prayer support.

The visual materials can include whatever can be imagined and fits the culture of the church. Some of the many pieces that have been developed include posters, banners, cups, t-shirts, hats, bumper stickers, money clips, refrigerator magnets, and peel-off stickers. These items usually have no more than the campaign title or logo in the appropriate colors. The purpose is to create a visual reminder that keeps the capital campaign in the minds of the members. One creative director developed a "Burma Shave" set of external posters for the primary walk between the parking lot and the church. The sequential message caught everyone's attention in a most unique way.

In some churches developing a brochure may be valuable. However, a well-done brochure is frequently expensive. Also brochures are often not the most effective way of communicating in a capital campaign. The fact sheet answers questions in a better way. The old idea that the brochure follows the outline of greeting from pastor and campaign director, history of the church, current ministry, need for the project with artist rendering or blueprints, and a motivation for response has largely been replaced with audio or video presentations and the use of the information booth.

Of course, there is a need for some simple graphic material such as note cards, a letterhead, commitment cards with privacy envelopes, major-event invitations and programs, and announcements in newsletters and bulletins about campaign meetings and activities.

Some copy needs to be developed for both newsletters and bulletin inserts. The regular church newsletter could be used for campaign information, but the information should not be overwhelmed by the rest of the church news. Bulletin inserts can include information about the major event, could present written statements of support, or could be used in the prayer-support effort.

Delivering the Information

The brochure has been replaced in many campaigns by the use of an information booth staffed by building-committee members who can answer questions. The booth includes the plans, the artist's rendering of a building, or other graphics. Visual materials could also be distributed from the booth. One church built a freestanding kiosk and moved it from one high-traffic area to another during the campaign. They included a video loop of testimonies and changed the printed material to fit the interests reflected in that particular traffic area.

Part of the communication plan could also be small-group meetings to make presentations or answer questions about particular aspects of the project or campaign. This is often helpful with people who may have concerns about debt issues and how the projects will affect them. In one church a massive renovation was being planned that had an impact on sixteen different floors of church buildings. While the senior adults were interested in the success of the campaign, many of them had a particular concern about the location of the new elevator and the expanded restrooms. A meeting with their Sunday school class relieved their anxiety when presented by one of their peers.

One additional possibility in the communication plan is the use of a video or audio cassette. If the church uses media presentations already, then this ought to be seriously considered. It also might be considered if media presentations are planned in the immediate future. However, if a video or audio presentation is used, it needs to be done with a level of professionalism and should not look like your slides of a long-ago vacation. Most often this is worth the expense of hiring a video production company for the production and the presentation. The expense can be significant, but if it touches one heart for one significant commitment, the value has been established. When some grandparents in a church saw the church video that featured their granddaughter's class at play in the church, their commitment grew from $5,000 to $30,000. The pastor felt the $10,000 spent on the eight-minute video had been a good investment.

The communication plan might also include the use of the Internet. Some churches have websites established and regular e-mail correspondence with their members. Of course, many churches do not have this capacity. If it fits the culture of the church, it ought to be used. In one campaign all meeting notices and special events were announced through e-mail. The attendance was higher than normal, which validated the Internet support.

Age is a significant issue in the development of the communication pieces. A seventy-year-old does not think like or have the same perspective as a forty-year-old, yet both will be members of the congregation needing the information from the communications team. And the twenty-five-year-old will have still another set of standards, values, and communication styles that the communications team must address. Children and youth must also be included, because a capital campaign is a unique opportunity to teach stewardship to the younger generation.

The communications plan can produce some significant costs. It is the responsibility of the communication director, with assistance from the professional campaign consultant, to contain costs. That usually means making wise choices about what integrated approach best informs and encourages the members.

Chapter Nine

Opportunities for Steps of Faith

The Importance of Major Gifts

For years, professional campaign consultants have used the theme "Not Equal Gifts but Equal Sacrifice" to address one of the most common misconceptions about capital campaigns. It is not unusual to hear a church leader say, "We need about one million dollars for our project, so we need two hundred families to commit five thousand dollars each over the next three years." That is good math and very logical, but it is not accurate and represents bad theology. It has been my observation that some of the largest church capital campaigns in history have occurred in the last twenty-five years. While several factors have influenced this result, the primary reason is major gifts by generous donors.

In the 1980's, the founder of a Fortune 500 corporation was a member of a church along with several of his children and grandchildren. This wealthy man was known for his philanthropy in the city where he lived and had given generously to projects across America. His church conducted a capital campaign to address seven million dollars of building projects. The pastor visited the man and challenged him to make a million-dollar commitment. The man responded with the commitment and a chapel was named for the man's mother and family.

A few years ago, a woman gave a $150,000 stock gift in a $2 million campaign in her church. A divorced single mother, modest in her lifestyle, she had been an early employee of a major computer company. As she advanced into a management position, she received and purchased stock. Now retired, she was grateful to the church for the way it had ministered to her and her children through the years.

A husband and wife in one church were active leaders, and the husband served on the building committee. Though not wealthy, they owned their own business and both had worked hard for its success. They were asked to co-chair their church's $3.5 million capital campaign. Because of their love and enthusiasm for their church's ministry to their two children, they decided very early in the campaign that they would give $25,000 to the campaign.

But they took seriously the challenge to pray about their commitment. He was a jogger, and in his early morning runs he would pray and think about their commitment. He remembered how his parents gave generously out of very limited resources for their church's building project. His wife also continued to pray about their commitment. She remembered how her grandmother had been so generous to others in a small-town church. The prayers of the husband and wife made a difference. They doubled their commitment to $50,000, then continued to pray and raised their commitment to $75,000 and finally to $100,000.

Several factors have contributed to this changing pattern for giving to the local church:

- Professional fundraising consultants have emphasized the importance of major gifts.
- Pastors and church leaders began asking for major gifts.
- A growing economy provided increased potential for significant giving.
- There has been an increased educational emphasis on the tax advantages of charitable contributions.
- More naming and memorial-gift opportunities have been identified in some churches.

Traditional fundraising efforts by institutions and community organizations have long recognized the need for major gifts. Often one-half to eighty percent of a campaign goal is received from major donors and campaign leaders. Even church-related institutions have been far ahead of local congregations in asking for major gifts and commitments. Wealthy church members have given major gifts to these efforts while giving nominal support to their local churches.

A growing church in the suburbs of a large metropolitan area had conducted several capital campaigns in its fifteen-year history. Faced with a critical need for both educational space and a new sanctuary, the plan was to address education space first and delay the sanctuary project. Encouraged by a professional consultant, the pastor visited with twelve potential top donors. They were challenged about their influence and ability. The visits with these twelve families resulted in commitment equal to the total costs projected for the sanctuary. The congregation then provided the commitments necessary for the educational needs. There was potential in the church for both projects, but it took some major gifts for the potential to be realized. If the church had planned to move forward without the effort by the pastor to cultivate some major gifts, the sanctuary project would have been delayed. Instead, the church was able to celebrate what seemed an almost miraculous result that provided for its continued growth.

Major Gifts in Your Congregation

There are two common refrains by church leaders about the possibility of major gifts in their church. First, leaders will say that their church just doesn't have any wealthy people. In most churches, however, one of every forty families has the ability to make a one-time gift that is equal to the church's annual budget (*Generous People,* by Eugene Grimm; Abingdon Press, 1992; page 118). Appearances can be deceptive, as the opening stories of this chapter indicate. Some leaders express their limited perception by saying that a lot of their members live on a fixed income. The truth is that some of their members are probably well fixed. Accumulated assets are far more important than discretionary cash flow for major gifts. Second, leaders acknowledge that there may be some potential for major gifts but say that these have never been realized before. This is one of the times when having a professional campaign consultant shows its value, for they bring tools like tested gift profile guides that can help. Experience shows that there is potential for major gifts in most congregations.

Asking for Major Gifts

Major gifts can usually be identified through the leader-commitment team. The pastor, campaign director, and leader-commitment director can usually develop a list of potential major donors based on their personal knowledge of the congregation. A key to major gifts is the role of the pastor in cultivating and soliciting them.

It is inconsistent for pastors to deal with the most intimate matters in a family's life, like birth, marriage, illness, death, moral failure, and ethical problems, but have a prohibition from being involved in the family's use of wealth. In reading the New Testament, we find that people of wealth had significant roles in the ministry of Jesus and in the life of the early church. A mature pastor will know how to challenge people with significant giving potential without compromising his or her relationship with the congregation. The "asking" is more than a request for money. It is a challenge and encouragement to celebrate the blessings of God in one's life and to make a difference in the church's mission and ministry. The invitation to give must be a spiritual as well as a financial challenge. A common way to ask for a major gift is to use a gift profile guide showing the level of gifts needed, identify a level or range of amounts a person might give, and ask the individual to pray about making a commitment at that level. That presents the challenge as both a spiritual process and a request for a specific financial level. In some cases when a pastor is unable or unwilling to fulfill this role, another staff member or a key lay leader might do so.

Using a Gift Profile Guide

A gift profile guide is a chart showing the gifts required to raise a specific amount of money. It is based on the experience of hundreds of campaigns and can be modified on the basis of the potential of the major donors in a particular church. This guide helps interpret what constitutes a major gift in a particular church and campaign. In most capital campaigns, the rule of thirds will apply. This rule suggests that about one third of the total raised will come from the top six to ten commitments, another third will come from the next twenty percent of the commitments, and the final third will come from the remainder of the commitments. Four illustrations of gift profile guides have been provided for campaigns of $300,000, $500,000, $1 million, and $2 million (Illustrations 1, 2, 3, 4).

The amount a church can raise will be considered in a subsequent chapter, but these gift profile guides have been used in actual campaigns. The left column shows the number of commitments needed at a particular level. The next column establishes the amount of each commitment needed. The third column gives the total amount needed at a specific gift level, and the fourth column gives the cumulative total. A common response of leaders is to look at the gift profile guide and suggest that their church will not have the top gifts but will likely have more of the middle range of gifts. If that is true then the church will not raise the amount indicated on the guide. This conclusion is not a matter of faith but rather a simple matter of math. Using the gift profile guides for $300,000 and $1 million, look at the actual results of the top gifts from some campaigns.

One church (#6 in Illustration 5) was a small rural congregation with an annual budget of about $125,000 from 130 families. Their project was new construction costing more than $300,000. They received eighty-four commitments that totaled $367,000. Their top nine gifts were:

- 1 at $31,391
- 1 at $25,000
- 1 at $20,000
- 1 at $18,000
- 2 at $15,000
- 1 at $12,000
- 2 at $10,000

These nine gifts accounted for $156,391 (42%) of the total raised.

A second church (#23 in Illustration 5) was in a small town and had 225 families and an annual budget of $237,000. Their project was also more than $300,000 for debt and some renovations. They received 130 commitments that totaled $372,000.

Their top ten gifts were:

- 1 at $40,000
- 1 at $27,000
- 1 at $16,000
- 1 at $15,000
- 1 at $14,400
- 1 at $13,500
- 1 at $12,000
- 1 at $10,500
- 2 at $10,000

These ten gifts resulted in $168,400, which was 45% of the total raised.

A third church (#32 in Illustration 5) was in the urban setting of a large city. It was an old church with a new innovative ministry and a need for major renovations. Their membership list was not very accurate, and their budget was just less than $400,000. They had a variety of phases in their renovation plans and wanted to raise as much as they could to meet those goals. They hoped to raise as much as $1 million. When the campaign concluded, they had received about two hundred commitments that totaled almost $1,225,000. Their twelve leading gifts were:

- 1 at $100,000
- 1 at $50,000
- 4 at $30,000

- 1 at $25,000
- 2 at $20,000
- 3 at $18,000

These twelve commitments added up to $389,000, or 32% of the total amount raised.

As shown in these examples, a gift profile guide can be a helpful tool. Identifying, cultivating, and soliciting major gifts in a church capital campaign offers disciples of Jesus Christ a challenge and an opportunity for taking some significant steps of faith.

Tax Advantages of Major Gifts

Many major gifts in capital campaigns are given through creative, tax-beneficial giving. The most common gift is the transfer of appreciated stock to the church. The donor avoids paying capital-gains tax and receives the full value of the stock at the time of transfer as a charitable contribution. Marketable and appreciated real estate, collectibles, and jewelry are also common in this kind of giving. Since the church will be selling these assets it is important that they are actually marketable.

The donor is responsible for determining the value of any asset gift, including an appraisal if required. The church simply acknowledges the receipt of the gift and sells the asset at whatever price the market will bear regardless of the appraised value. Churches should have a gift-acceptance policy so inappropriate gifts can be declined. An inappropriate gift could be an asset that is not marketable or has unacceptable conditions. For instance, land should be able to pass an environmental audit, and stock should be easy to liquidate and not need to be held. Churches have lost asset value by "playing the market." Since the laws concerning charitable contributions and tax consequences are changed from time to time, the donor should seek professional counsel before making the gift. It is not the church's responsibility to provide this counsel.

While the gift profile guide is a useful tool for helping church members understand the need for gifts and the kind of major gifts needed, it should never be allowed to limit their response. In one church a need for $3 million seemed overwhelming, and the lead gift needed was projected at $500,000. The pastor had been cultivating a key potential donor by providing information about the project and asking his counsel. The potential donor had made a fortune in the construction business. The pastor asked the consultant to go with him to visit the potential lead donor. After a casual conversation, the member asked what was needed for a lead gift. The man had been involved in a lot of capital campaigns for his alma mater and knew how campaigns worked. The consultant showed the man a gift profile guide that had the $500,000 gift listed as the lead. The church member asked if an answer was needed in this meeting. The consultant indicated that an answer was not needed for several weeks and asked if the man would simply pray about his involvement. Then the consultant challenged the man to consider making the largest gift he had ever made and to not be limited by the gift profile. Six weeks later the man made a commitment of $750,000 for the capital campaign and raised his annual commitment for the church budget to $100,000 a year. This substantial commitment was the result of a spiritual process in a man who had been richly blessed.

Chapter Ten

Let's Have a Party

The Churchwide Celebration

When David raised the resources to build the Temple, he gave a challenge to the assembly. In 1 Chronicles 29 the value of a strong and positive group dynamic can be seen. The project was explained to the whole assembly, the spiritual context was defined, the leaders made their gifts, and then there was a celebration.

Unfortunately, in the church today there is often a scarcity of celebrations and especially a shortage of times when the whole church is gathered at one time in one place. With multiple worship services and small-group ministries, church members sometimes have a difficult time developing a perception of how large their church really is. This can complicate the understanding of the need for facility and program expansion.

Having a major celebration event helps to build credibility during a capital campaign. It communicates that the church is doing something different, not just business as usual. The planning and program for a major event of the gathered church can involve a lot of people and challenge them about their own responses. The primary question today is not whether a church should have a major event in a capital campaign, but what it looks like in the context and culture of a particular church.

What Is a Major Event?

A major event is one of the climactic events in the campaign. It can provide the most memorable activity in a campaign for years to come. More importantly it can be used to encourage and prepare hearts for an optimum response spiritually and financially.

The practice used to revolve almost solely around a large church banquet, often at a hotel or convention center. While banquets afford a more formal opportunity for the church to gather, the changing culture began to challenge both the costs and formality. Also, time has become a challenge as well. With our contemporary culture demanding more and more in work, family, school, and even leisure pursuits, fewer people want to give up an evening for a church banquet. This is especially true of those people less motivated to make a financial commitment. Banquets still fit the culture of some churches, but there are a lot of other options available that have also proven to be effective. The central question is how we can create a special event that will yield maximum attendance.

Churches have experimented with a lot of models in recent years, including luncheons after church on Sunday, but the approach that more and more churches have been using is the planning of a special Sunday morning. It has not been unusual for churches to move their worship services to a convention center for Easter services or to a school when they have outgrown their sanctuary. In the same fashion, having a celebration service with a brunch on Sunday morning at a site other than the church has become very popular. Some churches have also found that having the event on-site with the use of large tents has created a festive spirit. As in so many aspects of a capital-campaign design, the right decision depends on the culture and history of the church. What might be just right for one church might not fit another congregation at all. The professional campaign consultant can offer further advice on designing the celebration event.

Planning the Event

If the church decides to have a Sunday morning activity, the leaders need a two-part planning sequence with regard to the program approach. It is usually more comfortable for the church to have a brunch and celebration in the first part of the program. This might feature celebrative music, children's activities, and drama presentations and be more of an entertainment venue. The details of this part of the program can be determined by the major-event directors along with the pastor and campaign director.

The hospitality team also assists with the major event. In addition to receiving reservations for the major event, the hospitality team can help serve food, clean up, park cars, reserve seats for senior adults, assist with directions, help with children, and greet people as they arrive.

The second part of the planning for the program is the approach to worship. In a time when churches have worship services that are traditional, contemporary, liturgical, reflective, and blended, the worship design for this event should reflect an approach that the majority of the people can appreciate. In the context of worship, the pastor should challenge the people about their commitments in the campaign. A large part of that challenge is the announcement of the total of the leadership gifts. Until the major event, some people have not really considered their own response specifically. There is a natural curiosity about the capacity of the church and the willingness to respond to a financial need that often sounds very daunting. An announcement of substantial leader commitments not only establishes credibility but also raises the level of response. In one church the multiple projects presented a significant financial challenge. When the leadership gifts were announced, it became apparent that with a little stretching by the rest of the people, the church could accomplish two more of the phases. The celebration did not stop with the major event. People came to the commitment day the next week with a high expectation of success.

One thing to consider when planning the event is whether or not to receive financial commitments in the context of the worship time. There is not one answer that is always right. Some feel that this is a time of high emotion and maximum attendance and the right time to respond. Others feel equally passionate that this is a preparation for one last week of prayer prior to commitment and is setting the stage for the best response. If commitments are to be received in a major-event setting, then any leader announcement or showing of a campaign video should be done the week prior to the major event. Both methods have proven successful in different churches.

Considerations for Huge Events

One last word about the major event is the spectacular event that some churches have used. Some larger churches in multimillion-dollar campaigns have planned huge events. One church found that no site for a major event was available in their community, so they rented a city park with an amphitheater and prayed for no rain. They had food stations throughout the site and realized an attendance of more than four thousand people. Another church hired a newly constructed symphony hall and had a major musical presentation as a part of their event. Music was a large part of the ministry of the church and this was a great idea for their membership. Many churches have hired convention centers and used buses to transport their people. These megaevents usually require additional consideration for matters such as on-site medical support, significant children's program planning, security, transportation, and parking. Of course each of these challenges affords another way to involve church members.

Chapter Eleven

Opportunities for Response

The Commitment Process

Not too long ago, there was a closely defined process for receiving commitments in a church capital campaign. A large organization was built for canvassing every member with a home visit. The purpose of the visit was to take a commitment card to the home, discuss the campaign, and solicit a specific financial commitment. By the time of the visit, every family had been evaluated in terms of their financial potential, and a recommended amount was actually written on the card prior to the visit. The prescribed commitments were determined by a committee using variables such as occupation, age, and neighborhood to derive a suggested figure. Furthermore, after the commitment was received, if a family fell behind, another group was assigned to visit them. In this era the word *pledge* was more common than *commitment*.

Of course, by today's standards, the process was very coercive and labor intensive. But culture changes with time and so must the process by which commitments are received. In contemporary society this process seems not only coercive but impractical. In a society as pressed for time as ours, it is more difficult to find families at home than it once was. As a matter of fact there has been recent research indicating that an attempt to canvass every member actually has a detrimental effect on individual response ("Patterns of Giving Among United Methodists," by Charles E. Zech, in *The People(s) Called Methodist: Forms and Reforms of Their Life,* edited by William B. Lawrence, Dennis M. Campbell, and Russell E. Richey; Abingdon Press, 1998; pages 91 and 100-101).

There are other significant cultural challenges, such as the eroding loyalty to both denomination and congregation from individuals. Communication has also been complicated in the contemporary culture of our churches. With erratic attendance from a great number of church members, it is far more difficult to develop a clear understanding of the corporate direction of the church. This lack of loyalty is further complicated by people who consider themselves adherents and not church members with implied responsibilities. With these challenges to the process, the central question becomes what we can do to elicit the highest number of responses in an individual church.

Incidentally, one way to evaluate a potential professional consultant is to inquire about his or her flexibility in the campaign design. If a consultant suggests that canvassing every member is the only choice, it may indicate that he or she has not stayed current with materials and approaches.

Commitment Is a Process

The commitment process has a variety of opportunities for participation and response. During the preparation phase as church leaders are making decisions about projects, costs, and funding, there also needs to be a prayer component. People need to be asked to pray for God's direction both for the church and for their individual parts in God's plan.

In the early stages of the process, cultivation of individual major commitments can begin. It is very easy for pastors or other key leaders to visit with individuals to solicit opinions and share critical information. This building of ownership can be very helpful in realizing major commitments later in the campaign.

In the enlisting and training of the steering committee, leaders and trainers can communicate the clear expectation of a financial response from committee members by a specific deadline. A common approach is to ask the steering committee for a tentative commitment early in the campaign. This provides the professional consultant with a barometer for the effectiveness of the communication and the strength of the steering committee.

Churches can also prepare the stage for response through the leader-commitment team. Individual meetings focus on coordinating the campaign as well as providing the opportunity for leaders to set the pace with an early response. Handing out commitment cards at leader-commitment gatherings and receiving them prior to the major event is a clear response opportunity.

The general receipt of commitment cards can begin with the major event or the subsequent commitment day. It is important that the people are informed and prepared for the response and that it is very intentional and well planned. If a response is expected at the major event, it needs to be communicated in promotion about the event, in the reservation calls, and from the pulpit. The leader-commitment announcement would need to be shared the week before the event for influence to be effective. And commitment cards should be both mailed in advance and available at the time of expected response. If a commitment day subsequent to the major event is used, the same preparation applies. And in the conclusion of the major event, a clear challenge should be issued about the importance of the week ahead and the expectation that all will come prepared to respond.

Commitment Day

The process that has developed for several months should culminate with a very holy time of response. Even if some have already responded with a commitment card as a part of the leader-commitment process or individual visits, the commitment day ought to be a time for everyone to publicly respond. While it is important to remember the vision and encourage a sense of ownership, the more important fact is that for many in the church, this will be the beginning point of a commitment to biblical stewardship. Of course, the worship time and the response time specifically ought to be supported in deep and thoughtful prayer.

Even though the commitment day should be preceded by a pastoral letter and commitment card, it is necessary in the service to allow time for card distribution to assure that everyone has a commitment card in hand. Those who forgot theirs can be given new ones, those who already turned one in can get another one to use symbolically, and those who brought their cards with them might want to change them.

The card needs to be explained during the commitment service. It is important that the card be simple, with one response that is clear. Asking people to also make a commitment to the annual budget, be available for service opportunities, or promise time to the prayer ministry is not appropriate during this time.

After reviewing the card it is best to offer a time of silence and reflection with soft music in the background. There are many ways to receive commitment cards. They can be received like an offering at the commitment time or they can be simply passed down the pews to the aisle and received by ushers; in either case, an envelope should be used for the sake of confidentiality. Many churches have asked members to bring their commitment cards forward to the front of the church. This demonstrative response is enhanced when a special table or response receptacle is used. Some of the most moving response times are when the people actually have to move. Whatever method is used, the regular offering and commitment time should not be combined.

In today's culture, we can expect half of our church members to be absent on any given Sunday. When we have a preannounced commitment day, we can count on attendance challenges. And the fact that a person is present doesn't mean he or she will be ready or willing to respond, despite the preparation. It is important that the nonrespondents be contacted with information and encouragement. In some settings, each one can be sent an individual handwritten note with an additional commitment card. This is particularly effective when peers contact people within their sphere of influence. If there are larger potential donors who have not yet responded, a contact from the pastor, campaign director, or leader-commitment director might be effective. Another possibility is to build a small organization of callers who will telephone nonrespondents. In all of these approaches the message should provide information about the result of commitment day, such as the number of responses, the amount of money committed to date, and the sense of celebration that was experienced. Then the message should encourage the person to participate. This can be done by simply expressing that the purpose of the call is to provide information and to let everyone know that in a couple of weeks an announcement will be made about the total and that responses therefore need to be in before then. If more than that is discussed, there is a risk of alienating the nonrespondent. An effective means of preventing this is to clearly state at the start of the campaign that not everyone will or can participate, but the more who do, the greater the benefit to the church will be.

The length of the financial commitment is also an issue in some settings. In the vast majority of capital campaigns, a three-year commitment is realistic and can offer flexibility for an early close or extension of the campaign. In some settings, a shorter time has been used. If the membership is particularly transient or if the need is less than two times the ordinary annual income of the church, a shorter time of commitment might be merited.

On the concluding Sunday of the campaign, it is important to make an announcement of the number of commitments made and the approximate amount of money committed to date. Language of closure should be soft and the invitation left open for additional commitments.

Chapter Twelve

Assuring Optimum Success

Completion and Follow-Up

After what is sometimes called Victory Day, the "victory" needs to be received. In other words, commitments need to be converted into cash. A campaign that has built in intensity through a major churchwide event and culminated in a commitment day and subsequent announcement of a commitment total that seemed impossible needs to end. The next phase is the completion and follow-up. The purpose of this stage should be to keep the program in front of people in a positive way without the same intensity as the campaign itself.

The question that is most often heard when a church is about to retain professional counsel is what kind of follow-up the consultant and company will provide. The accurate answer is that a professional consultant usually wants to do a lot more than the church leaders are willing to do.

The Confirmation Letter

The transitional activity from campaign to completion and follow-up is the use of a confirmation letter. Immediately after commitment day, the local church's financial office should issue a letter of confirmation to everyone who made a commitment in the campaign, whether the commitment was a specific dollar amount or just a positive response with no specific financial amount indicated. This letter affirms the specific commitment made, indicates the method by which the designated commitment will be received, and offers a phone number and name in the financial office as a contact to answer any remaining questions. This letter puts in front of the member the financial office's understanding of the commitment amount and terms. It is also a gentle reminder and means of accountability.

The Quarterly Report

The next step is to establish who has responsibility for follow-up. It is unrealistic to expect the professional consultant to continue to be the catalyst in the follow-up phase of the campaign. In past times, a designated follow-up director was enlisted, but this was seldom effective. It seems that the best people for follow-up are either staff or members of the building committee. This allows for better access to the facts necessary for an effective follow-up approach.

A cornerstone tool for follow-up is a quarterly report mailed to all of those who made a commitment or who have made gifts without a commitment. Those who have made neither a commitment nor any gift should be made aware that there is a report available if they are interested, but they will need to request it. There is no apparent value in sending the report to all church members. If people have indicated through lack of commitment or contribution that they have little interest in the project, then sending them information may be perceived as being confrontational.

The quarterly report should provide three kinds of information. First, it needs to offer an ongoing accounting of the money. Information such as the number of commitments, the amount received from pledges, and the gifts received that were not pledged should be reported as revenue, and the expenses should be generally summarized. Second, the report should give a clear explanation of the status of the project since the last report. If there have been change orders, changes in design or materials, problems, or changes in costs, the people who have made commitments need to know. One of the worst things that can happen in follow-up is limited communication about changes in the finances through change orders, construction-cost overruns, or changes in major commitments. The third focus of the quarterly report should be encouragement. This can be a further expression of a statement of support, an analysis of cost savings from construction decisions, or the amount saved by interest on commitments or a lower interim interest rate.

A common problem with producing a quarterly report is not being timely. There seems to be an enormous tendency to wait for something to happen before a report is issued. Timeliness will allow the piece to be shorter in content, and if it is sent with a distinctive color or masthead for identification, people will become used to its purpose. Even if nothing has happened due to labor problems, material delays, or weather issues, that should be reported.

Providing Ongoing Information

Verbal presentations can also be used to provide continuing information. Regular verbal presentations seem to work best when additional decisions need to be made or reported. If the construction process leads to additional costs or even more dramatic project changes, it is absolutely imperative that these changes be presented and discussed. To have a capital campaign for one project and then, after commitments have been made and contributions have begun, to significantly change the project without informing the donors is a major integrity issue and can have extremely negative effects on church life as well as commitment receipts. While this seems logical to most leaders, it takes an intentional effort, specific assignments to people, and additional energy to continue to communicate effectively.

There are a number of times in addition to the occurrence of something unexpected when a report, further solicitation, and celebration can help the follow-up. Groundbreaking for a new building can be a significant event, as can the beginning or expansion of new programs and activities. Part of the encouragement section of the quarterly report can include ministry enhancements made possible by the capital campaign. Some churches also like to have a consecration service when a new facility is first opened, and this can be reported as well.

Whether the church has paved a parking lot, opened an educational building, or removed old temporary facilities, there is an opportunity for follow-up communication. One church demolished some old facilities in order to build a new and larger educational wing. In the process of demolition, a five-story bell tower was preserved for the final act of demolition. The removal of the tower and the building of a new facility was actually going to change the skyline of the town. The church used the final demolition as a community event with television coverage and substantial church publicity. The act of demolition was a real transition of direction for the church. Other opportunities such as one-year, eighteen-month, two-year, and two-and-a-half-year milestones in a three-year commitment process afford special times of verbal and visual reporting and can relate to opportunities for new-member involvement and campaign renewals and extensions.

Involving New Members

Involving new members who join the church after commitment day is a particular challenge in which assumptions seldom prove accurate. A lot of professional consultants will indicate that new members should be assimilated in the capital campaign as they join or in new-member gatherings scheduled every few months. The truth is that new members seldom make commitments, much less substantial commitments, in this way.

In personal dialogue over the last twenty-five years, pastors have often told me that new members in their churches seldom begin their memberships with strong financial support. To think that a member will come to a church and immediately make commitments to support the regular offering and special offerings and then make a substantial commitment over and above this to a building project that he or she does not own yet is an assumption that disappoints many. The most effective way to involve new members has been to use renewal times once or twice in the course of the three-year commitment process. This is especially effective if the rest of the church is also offered a time to renew their commitments. This builds some of the group dynamic found in the original campaign and creates a churchwide expectancy that allows for some ownership to develop.

Can Capital Campaigns Be Extended?

In some campaigns the results, subsequent increases of costs, and even significant changes in the economy merit the consideration of an extension or additional campaign. The issue of an additional campaign will be discussed later, but the campaign extension can be used as an effective follow-up.

In one church, the project costs were estimated, the annual budget was trimmed to allow additional debt, and the capital campaign raised about $2.5 million. When the bids and actual construction costs began to come in and all of these factors were evaluated at eighteen months into the giving cycle, it was apparent that the church needed at least an additional $400,000 to complete everything. The decision was made to have a renewal at thirty months, when all those who had made commitments that were to be completed in six months were asked to review their commitments and consider extending them for an additional twelve months. New members who had not made commitments were asked to consider making a commitment for eighteen months, representing both the remaining time on the original campaign and the extension.

A simple fact sheet was provided. Meetings were conducted in which families who were being challenged to extend their giving discussed their commitments with those new members who were being asked to make a commitment for the first time. The campaign video was updated and shown in worship service, and three weeks of sermons and testimonies highlighted the effort. This took six weeks from planning to commitment and resulted in an additional $600,000 in commitments. Almost one third of the new commitments came from new families. Renewal and extension have been used in several settings with similar results. But this is not always the best solution; if the need is for more than about 25% of the original commitments, a campaign extension is usually not advised.

Maintaining Credibility

Effective ongoing communication during the entire follow-up period increases the percentage of commitments being fulfilled and supports the positive spirit of the capital campaign. When a church reaches the end of a commitment time and members receive the surprise of unexpected debt or a significantly different project, credibility suffers.

Ongoing communication can also address other possibly negative influences such as staff changes, the loss of membership, and community issues. One strange development in some churches is a spirit of revisionist history. After the campaign, following changes in staff, pastoral leadership, and project, some begin to remember the campaign in imaginative, nonfactual terms. When one church needed to have a capital campaign for a new building, some members recalled that the campaign led by a professional eight years before had really not been a good experience. When asked why, they said their project had been changed, their pastor had left, and it had taken longer to build than it should have. They attributed these negative factors to the professional consultants who had concluded their service prior to any of these problems. Effective communication in follow-up can help the church have a more accurate memory.

Chapter Thirteen

How Much Can We Raise?

Analysis of Potential

Several years ago a church contacted a consulting firm regarding the need for a major capital campaign. As the consultant asked about the details, the pastor of the church said that he had a core of leaders who were willing and capable of substantial commitments and that their vision called for forty million dollars in capital projects. The pastor also indicated that they were eager to move forward and wanted to know what the fee for the project would be. The consultant asked for a little more information and found that the church was only six months old, was meeting in a garage, and had a monthly income of about five thousand dollars. Their vision and optimism exceeded reality. A consideration of several factors is necessary to determine the giving potential of a church, including the experience of other churches. While faith is an issue, experience cannot be discounted.

Many times a committee in the process of selecting professional counsel or in the process of considering architectural plans and cost projections for a project overlooks the congregation's giving potential and trusts ambiguously in faith to make everything work. This reaction usually comes more from a consumer culture than from faith. Plans may need to be revised and downsized if they exceed realistic potential of what a capital campaign and safe debt would allow. When selecting counsel, it is also tempting to choose the consultant based on whether they say that the church can raise the amount needed. The disappointment that follows is borne not by the consultant but by the leaders who bought what they wanted to hear rather than what the facts suggested.

Another difficulty is discerning the difference between the need and the giving potential. The cost of a project has little to do with the potential or willingness to give. The financial goal of the campaign is not the anticipated cost of the projects, but rather raising as much as possible toward the need. While it is rare to raise more than needed, it does happen. The question is, if the project cost is not the goal, what is the basis of the gift profile guide? The guide can be determined by blending the need and the potential based on the expectations developed from experience and the giving potential of the church.

Learning From Others' Experience

Over the years major stewardship consulting firms have established a market expectation of potential based on their experience of designing and implementing thousands of programs across the country. In a three-year capital campaign, most churches can expect to raise from one and one-half to three times their previous year's budget receipts. In other words, if a church received $200,000 in budget receipts, the expectation in a capital campaign would be for the church to raise between $300,000 and $600,000. The difference between the low and high ends of the range is determined by major gifts and the base of support. In this illustration, if the church's need was for a $400,000 project and no known large gifts were identified early in the campaign, the gift profile guide would probably be developed for $400,000 to $500,000 with a lead gift of $50,000 to $75,000. This ratio analysis has proven useful and remarkably accurate, as the figures in Illustration 5 indicate. A particular church can look to the experience of other churches to develop a general idea of potential commitments; there are, however, other factors that can add to this analysis of potential.

Analyzing Demographic Information

One of the most basic factors used in analyzing potential is demographic information about the congregation. The number of resident families, the number of single heads of households, median age, and attendance are all indicators of potential. It is also important to consider the general level of income in the congregation. In one church, well over half the congregation worked at a specific factory that was the driving force in the local economy. More than 90% of the church members were hourly wage earners. Despite great faith, there was a limitation of available resources.

Resource potential is another factor that makes a difference. The previous year's income and giving patterns could be an indicator of potential. People who have the means to make major gifts can impact potential. Having high-income business and professional people who are faithful givers and having people who could give stock or land helps increase potential. Some young adults have been recipients of stock options and have a capacity that exceeds their income indicator. It is not unusual for a young adult to make a gift of $25,000 to $50,000 based on stock rather than income level.

The Church's Culture

The history of giving in a church also has a bearing on what might happen in a capital campaign. The experience in previous capital campaigns, special offerings, and even per capita giving indicate what could happen. If stewardship has been a strong factor in the teaching and expression of congregational life, the likelihood is that a capital campaign will be more successful.

The commitment of the leaders, the pastor, and the church to the project are strong factors that can create a climate of giving and expectation in a capital campaign. If the whole church (members, pastors, and staff) is united behind the project, a higher potential is likely. However, if some leaders or the pastor or staff members do not demonstrate support, it can have a very negative impact on the results.

The issue of the unity of the congregation is critically important. The spirit of the church reflected in the enthusiasm of church members about the church's program and ministry can make or break a campaign.

Some Examples

It is important to see a few examples of how these variables can impact the results as shown in Illustration 5. For instance, one question often asked is whether a particular type of project raises more funds than another. A general rule suggested by the results in the illustration is that churches will raise more for building new facilities or even buying land than they will for debt or renovation. The difference is striking and could impact the planning process. The average amount raised in these fifty campaigns was a little more than two and one-half times (252%) the previous year's income. However, when analyzed on the basis of debt or renovation compared to new construction, new construction averaged raising 270% and debt/renovation averaged 180%. In other words, if a church with a $200,000 annual income had a campaign for debt or renovation they could expect to raise about $320,000; but, if they raised money for new construction, the average expectation for the same church would be $540,000. If the building is constructed before the money is raised, the amount needed becomes debt, which will generate less of a response during a campaign. That would suggest that conducting the capital campaign before building would yield a lot more money, validating a delay in construction or better advance planning by the church. There are always exceptions, such as church #32, which raised more than three times their previous year's income. In this case the other factors mentioned were all very strong. There was a great deal of unity, there were major gifts available and realized, and there was a broad base of participation.

Another question that can be analyzed on the basis of experience is what it takes to exceed the ratio expectations. Sometimes a church needs to raise more than three times its income to validate a project. Fourteen of the fifty campaigns raised more than three times the church's annual income, and three of the campaigns raised more than four times the annual income. In every case, the difference was in major gifts. For instance, in church #43, the church raised $2,524,767 with a previous year's income of less than $590,000. The counsel had suggested a capacity of $1.5 million to $1.8 million if major gifts could be committed. The campaign realized all of the necessary major gifts and was on track for the upper end of the potential until one family, challenged to make a substantial gift, committed $750,000. Their gift made the difference between a good campaign of just less than $1.8 million and an extraordinary campaign of more than $2.5 million. When exceptions on the upper end of the range are experienced, one or two gifts are most often the difference.

Reviewing all of the factors, the experience of other churches, and the faith of the congregation, you can project some parameters that help frame realistic expectations.

Chapter Fourteen

Should We Borrow?

Safe Debt/No Debt

Math is often challenging. For instance, a church with a $250,000 annual income was told by their architect that their project to build a family life center was going to cost about $500,000. The church had no debt and conducted a successful capital campaign and received commitments of $500,000. They began their project six months into the receipt of the commitments, and their budget grew at about 5% a year over the course of the three years of capital campaign receipts. At the end of three years the church discovered it could not afford all of the debt it had incurred. How did this happen? On the surface it seems improbable, but a closer look will reveal the causes.

The nightmares that churches have had because of building programs usually are realized a few years down the road when the residual debt is not understood and is not affordable within the constraints of budget income. This has led some people to a philosophy that churches should never have debt. This is communicated by a number of church financial experts who base their feelings on a rather narrow interpretation of biblical principles. However, there is enough truth in these principles and enough illustrations like the one above to generate a great amount of emotion. And unfortunately, some churches do express more faith in lending institutions than they do in God. So is debt something to be avoided at all costs? Or is it perfectly acceptable and nothing to be concerned about? The truth lies somewhere between these two points of view.

We have the advantage of being able to draw conclusions from the experience of other churches as well as from the facts. Most of the major ministries in the country have used debt as a tool in growing ministries and providing for capital needs. God's blessing was not removed from these churches that handled debt responsibly.

However, there have been some awful examples of churches who borrowed on the basis of a commercial lender's underwriting when the lender did not have a good understanding of a church's economy. Most commercial lenders will review the church's annual budget and the value of the church's assets and not really consider the potential of the church to assimilate the loan repayment into their operational budget. However, institutions that regularly loan to churches understand how churches are different and have developed tools to project a "safe debt" for them.

Another logical response to the never-borrow attitude is to analyze what constitutes good stewardship. If a church waits until the money is in hand, several years could pass. But if the ministry is growing, the need is acute, and the construction costs are escalating, is it still good stewardship to delay until they have all the money? A number of churches that have waited have found the results to be increased costs of construction, the loss of momentum in church growth, and an eroding spirit within the church.

Cash-Flow Analysis

A tool called cash-flow analysis, seen in Illustrations 6 and 7, can reveal what happened to the church mentioned at the beginning of the chapter. The annual income of the church is shown with no debt service or cash on hand for the building. The church conducted the capital campaign and received $500,000 in commitments projected over a three-year time period. It has been my experience that on average, churches in a capital campaign receive about 85% of the amount made in pledges. There are certainly exceptions, but the average is needed for a conservative projection. Eighty-five percent of $500,000 is $425,000. Although the architect projected a cost for the project of $500,000, there were some contingency costs such as architect fees, site preparation, and cost increases due to a few change orders during construction. And some of the bids came in a little higher than projected since original bids from before the capital campaign were only good for 90 to 120 days. The average contingency costs are about 15% of the project cost. In this example that adds $75,000 to the price of the project. So now the cost is $575,000 and the income from the capital campaign is $425,000, a difference of $150,000.

The church proceeded with the project after six months of receiving capital-campaign receipts. The project took six months to complete. During the three years the church's annual budget income grew by an average of 5% a year. The church committed one third of the annual budget increase to future debt service. As seen in Illustration 6, in 2001 a debt service of $4,163 is established, which is 33% of the total budget increase of $12,500. Each year allows for another third of budget increase to be added to debt service. The result of this analysis suggests that the church is able to service a debt of $114,424 but they will have an actual debt of $205,355. (The cash flow including the loan amortization is detailed in Illustration 7.)

If church leaders have not budgeted carefully and communicated effectively with their people in the follow-up sequence of the capital campaign, the facts and figures could even be worse. The average church member will remember that the project cost $500,000 and that $500,000 was committed in the capital campaign. When they hear at the end of three years that the church is in debt that cannot be serviced, a major problem has been created. This is not an unusual story.

The cash-flow analysis can help church leaders as well as lenders to accurately project a safe debt limit. The church might need to have a campaign extension or revise their budget to increase the potential debt service. The project might need to be trimmed or delayed a few months. Another campaign might be needed after the initial campaign. There are many ways to resolve the challenges indicated, but they first must be analyzed.

Effect on Regular Giving

Another fear about the issue of safe debt is the impact of a capital campaign on the regular giving of a church. The usual term of commitment for a capital campaign is three years. This has historically seemed to work best. It gives flexibility to end the campaign after two years if receipts have been received early or to extend for a fourth year if the costs require it. The good news is that a capital campaign rarely has a negative impact on regular giving. In fact the opposite is true. In most cases, an effectively designed and implemented capital campaign has a significant positive influence on the regular giving in subsequent years. Most exceptions to this are the result of a few individuals who have given substantially to the annual effort and decrease their annual support in order to make a major gift to the capital campaign. One pastor complained that the budget had declined several thousand dollars the year after the campaign and demanded an answer from the consultant.

When the consultant analyzed the facts, two individuals who had given almost 25% of the total budget the year before the campaign had decreased their giving. They had made capital campaign commitments of several hundred thousand dollars while still being the two largest givers to the regular budget. When the results from those two donors were factored out, the remaining church members actually had a 6% increase in annual giving.

When churches choose to do a self-led capital campaign instead of hiring a professional consultant, however, there is frequently a decrease in subsequent annual giving. It is not unusual for a church that has led their own campaign to experience a plateau or decline of regular giving for two or three years.

Chapter Fifteen

Only If You Want to Succeed

The Use of Professional Counsel

Several years ago a suburban church with an annual budget of $400,000 needed almost $1 million for the purchase of additional land and the construction of an educational building. The pastor had observed several pastor friends whose churches had each had a professionally led capital campaign. The pastor decided that he knew enough and would commit the time to design and direct the campaign himself. Despite his best efforts, the campaign resulted in only $200,000 in commitments over three years. Since that was not enough for the projects, three years passed. During the three years the church did commit to purchasing the available land with a loan but could not buy all that they needed.

The church still had a critical need for additional educational space and borrowed more money to begin the projects. Based on their unsuccessful campaign, they decided to hire a professional consulting firm to assist them in a new capital campaign, although some members were not in favor because the fee was $30,000. During the course of their self-led three-year campaign, their budget had stopped growing. So three years later they still had a budget of just over $400,000. As the building project began, they were led through a capital campaign. Despite the reservation of some members, they committed more than $800,000 in the professionally led campaign. Their budget also began to grow again after the capital campaign. With building projects completed, the capital campaign completed, and the budget increasing again, the church began to grow. More than 90% of the capital campaign commitments were received during the three-year commitment time, and the budget grew in three years from a little more than $400,000 to a little more than $600,000.

Their community and church had grown during this three-year time period, and since their original plans had been delayed, they faced the need for additional land and buildings. Despite the experience of running two previous campaigns with obviously different results, they determined to do a new capital campaign without professional counsel. Their rationale was that they had now been trained, they could adapt their previous materials, everyone realized the need, some older people were still upset about spending money for a consulting fee, and they had some members who were really committed to providing leadership. So they designed and implemented a capital campaign without help. About one year into their three-year campaign, they asked me to make a consultative visit to review some challenges they were facing. When asked about their history, they told me about the first two campaigns and then spoke about their most recent self-led campaign with real pride. They said their people were happy, the materials were as good as the professional's, and they had saved all the money they would have spent on a big fee. When asked about the level of commitments and the challenges they were facing, they hesitantly said that they had raised about $300,000 in commitments and their annual giving had stopped growing. They didn't have enough money to proceed and the debt was going to cause them to stop missions funding and possibly eliminate a staff position. They had saved a fee of $30,000 but had raised $500,000 less than before and had damaged their budget giving! I counseled them to call off the self-led effort at eighteen months and conduct a professionally led campaign for debt. They reluctantly agreed, and despite debt being the least effective motivation in campaigns, their professionally designed and directed campaign resulted in just over $1 million in commitments to reduce their debt.

During this period of time, three different pastors came and went, and the church got into the position of being behind the curve in providing facility and program needs. The transitions of pastor and staff along with limitations on programs hurt this church's mission of ministry for almost a decade. This is an actual story, and the story is not all that unique. Sincerity does not replace competence or historical experience. Should churches hire professional assistance? Only if they want to succeed.

Objections to Professional Consultants

Why do church leaders routinely reject the idea of hiring help? Most think that the task is not that difficult. Others think that everyone else has their level of knowledge and commitment. Some have a problem with the perceived high costs of professional assistance. Many have fear of the unknown and imagine that a professional consultant will advocate a high-pressure approach. A few remember a bad experience with using help. In presenting a professionally led campaign to an older downtown church, one consultant heard the members talking about how bad the last campaign had been. Many of the members were shaking their heads in agreement, evidently remembering the harsh experience and horrors embellished with time. When asked about the campaign, they could not remember the exact date, but it was either forty or forty-two years earlier. The consultant agreed that to be remembered with such emotion so many years later, it must have been pretty bad.

Why Use a Professional Consultant?

It is very difficult to redirect revisionist history or confront well-intentioned emotional arguments. What is needed is an understanding of why professional help is the best approach and how to make a good choice from the many consultants available. There are some factors that confirm the wisdom of using a consultant to help meet challenging financial needs in a church.

Most churches do not have the staff or members with the time and expertise to design and direct an effective campaign. The task usually falls to the senior pastor, who has not been trained for, usually has no particular expertise in, and doesn't have the time to design and lead this effort. The pastor who attempts this can also compromise his or her pastoral role with some members. Members who have experience in fund development are often asked to help, but the church needs a capital stewardship program, not an institutional capital funds campaign. The missing ingredient is often the theological foundation.

The results indicate the need for help. In the illustration considered earlier, the church raised about 50% of their campaign projection at the cost of budget growth. Most consultant-led programs will raise at least two times the previous year's income. As a matter of fact, exceptions to this are very rare. When a church has raised two or more times their previous year's income in a self-led campaign, several factors have usually influenced the result. These have included a long-tenured and beloved pastor or a founding pastor as well as extraordinary lead gifts that have carried the results to success. In one case, the founding pastor, who had served twenty years, led an effort without professional help and raised almost exactly two times their previous year's income. It is interesting to note that they had experienced several consultant-led campaigns prior to this effort, and when they had a major campaign after this one, they again hired help. In another campaign, the need was almost $5 million, and the patriarch family made a commitment of $3 million to begin the campaign. In this case also, in the next campaign the church hired professional help. These stories are the rare exceptions, not the experience that most churches can expect.

An experienced stewardship consultant can bring spiritual focus as well as objectivity to the campaign. If a church does its homework and makes a good match with the consultant, at the end of the campaign the distinctive results will be the spiritual impact as well as the amount committed.

An experienced consultant also provides a well-organized and proven plan that can be adapted to the cultural distinctives of the church. This results in broadening the base of participation and support as well as raising the levels of major gifts.

The objectivity a professional consultant brings is valuable when combined with the positive infrastructure of accountability that he or she can build. The completion of assignments and the meeting of deadlines are critical to the success of a campaign. Staff and members are usually too busy with other responsibilities to concentrate on these details.

Finally, the tendency in the self-led effort is to cut some corners and to not fully understand the importance of some of the principles of the campaign. The shortcuts usually include not addressing the major gift needs and reducing the level of expectation; not meeting deadlines or completing assignments; not involving enough people; and trying to add the program as just one of a variety of ongoing church activities. The result of every one of these shortcuts is to diminish the level of participation.

Choosing the Right Consultant

The key to a good consultant-led campaign is choosing the right consultant. In some cases when there is a large faction against hiring a professional, an individual member will underwrite the fee as a part of her or his campaign commitment. In most cases the positive leadership of the pastor and church leadership can overcome these emotional objections.

Selecting a professional consultant is one of the most important decisions a church will make in the capital campaign. The choice is made more difficult by the proliferation of companies and people who have entered the field of stewardship consulting. Just as it is not appropriate to be proud of your humility, a professional consultant should not imply that her or his approach is more "spiritual." Be cautious about hiring such a person. Here are some questions that will also enable church leaders to make a good selection:

- Who will be the on-site consultant responsible for the campaign?
- How many years of experience does the company have?
- How many years of experience does the consultant have?
- How many campaigns has the consultant led in churches similar in membership and annual budget to ours?
- How many campaigns has the consultant led in churches of our denomination similar to ours? When? Where?
- How much time will the campaign take?
- What is the best time of the year to conduct a campaign? How will the schedule for the campaign be developed?
- Will the consultant lead other campaigns at the same time as ours? If so, how many?
- How will church members be used in the campaign?
- How will the campaign be developed and implemented to employ the unique features, distinctive needs, and particular circumstances of our congregation?
- How will the communications approach be developed in the campaign and what are the projected costs of this?
- How will response be encouraged? What will happen with non-respondents?
- What kind of follow-up to the campaign will be provided?
- What will the consultant or company do for the church during the three-year giving period?
- Are there additional costs for follow-up?
- How are goals set and who sets them?
- What are the fees, how are they paid, and can we have a thirty-day buy-out clause if we are not happy?
- Identify the last three campaigns directed by the consultant. With whom may we discuss those campaigns?

The strange truth is that many churches do not do good homework on the potential consultant and accept the sales presentation as the sole criteria by which to make a decision. The tragic result is hiring someone who can sell effectively but cannot deliver the best on-site consultation. Some of the larger companies actually send in marketing representatives to sell to the church and then make an assignment of consultant subsequent to the contract. The argument of the companies is that this allows them to assign the consultant who best matches the congregation. The truth is often that they can assign the best match for the company in terms of which consultant needs a campaign assignment and which consultant might already be working in the same geographical area. This saves the company travel expenses. This is also a very effective sales strategy. If a church is hearing presentations from three or four consulting companies and one of them sends a salesperson, the salesperson can suggest that the church also meet with a consultant from the same company. The church will then be hearing two presentations from that company and only one from each of the other companies. This gives that company the advantage and can often secure the deal for them. The key for the selection committee is to ask the questions and do their homework. This will increase the possibility of making the best match.

In the private sector there are at least three types of consulting firms. There are large national firms that specialize in capital and annual stewardship programs in churches; there are regional firms with the same focus that serve a specific region; and there are small "mom and pop" firms that usually feature a sole proprietor with some part-time assistance available. In each kind of firm there are some effective consultants, but each can also offer some limitations. The advantages of a large firm are a broader selection of consultants, perhaps more supporting resources, and an established track record that can be investigated. The disadvantages can be higher cost; a more standardized, less flexible approach; and consultants who work too many campaigns at one time. Regional firms are often a good value with more flexibility, better costs, and fewer ongoing campaigns; but the disadvantages can be inadequate back-up from company personnel and fewer resources available. The smaller firms can be the best or worst of values. The advantage is often a very experienced person who will be more affordable, more flexible, and will give more time to the effort. The disadvantage is a lack of accountability within the company for results and for keeping materials relevant and updated. The small company also sometimes has trouble providing back-up with the same level of experience. Again the key is doing the homework and determining the best match of consultant and church. Ultimately, the most important question is the match between the individual consultant and the church. The fee, the size of the company, and the depth of available resources are all secondary to who will be working with you and how she or he will relate to your people.

It is important to know that the people who serve as professional stewardship consultants are most often spiritually motivated men and women with integrity and professional training. They pay a significant price for their profession in travel time and lifestyle in order to serve. They deserve respect.

Should a church hire professional counsel? They should only hire counsel if they want to succeed. The one possible exception is the capital campaign in churches with annual incomes less than $100,000—a challenge that will be discussed in a later chapter.

Chapter Sixteen

Spending Money to Make Money

The Costs of a Campaign

The very heart of the idea of stewardship is management of resources and getting the best value for dollars spent. That is why the costs related to a capital campaign often raise a lot of concerns. From the decision to use a professional consultant to the type of communications and major event to have in the campaign, it is easy to spend money in the pursuit of the best campaign. The cost centers of the campaign (besides the cost of a professional consultant) are communications, food, and the major event. Communications, leader-commitment, and major-event directors ought to route their expenditures through the campaign director.

Communications Costs

Communications costs include not only the printing and distribution of materials but also the possibility of producing a video. In campaigns with goals of one million dollars or more, it is often advisable to consider producing a video. Sometimes there are resources available within the church to produce quality video and printed materials. With both print and video it is important to meet deadlines. Sometimes when a printer or a video production person is contributing services, he or she feels less pressure to meet deadlines; there is often value in contracting with professionals outside the church. The printed and video materials can be used through the entire commitment period of three years for follow-up, and if the video is done well, a different ending can be used to convert it into a tool for evangelism or new-member orientation.

Common sense also should be applied to these costs. Spending more money for artistic expression can backfire. In most churches an expensive sixteen-page color brochure will not raise any more commitments than a four-page fact sheet. On the other hand, if the printed material reminds you of a mimeograph machine from the 1950's, then you probably have not invested enough in the printed pieces.

Food Costs

Throughout the campaign there are opportunities for providing food. Some churches cannot have a meeting without having snacks available. There is not a biblical mandate that we have to eat every time we meet. There are, though, a few times when food is very appropriate. For instance, when leader-commitment meetings are held in a home, it is natural to have some sort of food. This could be anything from a full meal to dessert. It is usually effective for the leader-commitment director to get three bids from local caterers at a couple of consistent price points like seven dollars and ten dollars a head. This affords some choices and contains the costs. Of course leaders also need to consider the cost of serving, paper goods, and clean-up. The other major food cost is for the major event. The design of the event will dictate food needs, but the process of receiving bids should be approximately the same.

Major-Event Costs

The major event can also generate expenses for location rental, tent rental, children's activities including childcare, any special youth activities, necessary transportation costs, and possibly the provision of medical and security services. This event will be a significant cost, but in relation to the amount being raised, the costs are virtually negligible. This event will not work if it is a covered-dish dinner or if it looks like every other event the church has. (A possible exception is in smaller churches.) The event needs to be enjoyable and memorable. The major-event director should work with the campaign director and the pastor on the budget.

Cost of Professional Counsel

The most controversial cost will be the fee for professional counsel. Illustration 8 is a chart of approximate commercial fees entering the twenty-first century. The value of the counsel is addressed in the previous chapter, but there are also some ways that these costs can be handled. It is not unusual for a church that has never used professional counsel to let the issue of the cost stop the momentum toward a capital campaign. No amount of logic can overcome a few emotional and strident voices in a congregational meeting. To reduce the controversy, many churches invite some individual or individuals to underwrite the campaign fee. This usually quells the negative sentiments. It is also advisable to review the contract closely. The contract should be based on a flat fee, usually based on the budget and membership of the church, not the size of the project or the amount of money to be raised. It is unethical to charge a percentage of the amount raised because it would compromise the leadership of the consultant and would have to be paid from commitments and not receipts. No reputable company charges on that basis. The payment schedule, and in some cases the fee, can be negotiated. The usual practice is for the fee to be paid during the course of the campaign prior to commitment day with a payment or two remaining after commitment day. This is fair to both the church and the consultant. If the church wants the consultant to have an on-site presence for follow-up at certain intervals, it should be included in the contract and paid for upon receipt.

When all of the costs are tallied at the end of a major capital campaign, they seldom exceed 5% of the amount raised. This is a good value for services received in every area. Identifying some of the cost savings can provide good copy for a newsletter article during the campaign. Most churches that have had several campaigns understand that the costs are simply the cost of doing business and are a good value. On the other side of the issue is the church discussed in the last chapter that decided after an "expensive" campaign that raised $800,000 and cost almost $30,000 that they should do their own campaign and save some money. The result was a total commitment of only $300,000—but they did save all that money. The cost of saving the money was $500,000 plus delayed projects.

Chapter Seventeen

Handling Common Problems

Capital Campaign Challenges

It is not unusual for church leaders to have unrealistic expectations about a capital campaign led by a consultant. One such expectation is that there will not be any problems if they hire someone to lead the campaign. Another source of disappointment is unrealistic assumptions about the amount that can be raised, assumptions based on the need rather than the capacity and willingness of the people. Sometimes, there is disappointment about the response of particular individuals. When an affluent member buys a $200,000 recreational vehicle during a campaign and makes a commitment of $5,000, pastors can become discouraged. When a church is enlisting steering-committee members, sometimes a potential leader will not only decline to serve but express opposition to the campaign or project. Whether we have a good campaign depends on how we handle some of these challenges.

When a consultant is selected, one of the first things that usually takes place is a pastor-preparation meeting. This is an attempt to set the right foundation from the beginning of the campaign. You can circumvent a lot of possible problems if you give this meeting the time necessary. Issues like campaign design and calendar commitments can be discussed and conflicts can be reduced. You can work out the role of the pastor, including the enlistment of the steering committee and the pastor's personal financial commitment. Preparation of the pastor and the effective enlistment and training of the steering committee can prevent many of the more serious challenges in a campaign.

Of course, there are some problems that may not be anticipated. One of the more serious problems is disharmony in the congregation. If the church is experiencing controversy not related to the capital campaign, it can seriously damage the direction of the campaign. For instance, after beginning a campaign, one church discovered a serious conflict had emerged between two key staff members. The campaign was put on hold while the congregation addressed this problem. When the campaign resumed a few months later, the matter had been resolved and the campaign was successful. Disharmony can arise from a staff conflict or a conflict between factions in the church. Sometimes it is better to postpone the campaign, and at other times it is better to just press on with the campaign. This decision ought to be made by the pastor and church leaders with regard to the spiritual unity and mission objectives of the church and the campaign.

Another problem is assuming too much. The assumption that church members are well informed about the campaign plans is seldom accurate. The unfounded belief that the congregation can meet a specific high financial goal can be a serious problem. If a church sets too high a goal and falls a few thousand dollars short, it can develop a lasting feeling of defeat. One suburban church set a goal at the level of the need despite the consultant's counsel that their project would probably require at least a one-year extension or, more probably, a second campaign. When they fell short of their need by $300,000, which could have been raised in an extension, the church leaders cancelled the project. The spirit of the church still suffers because of this "all-or-nothing" kind of attitude by the leadership.

Sometimes in the enthusiasm of a campaign, the leadership shows favoritism to those who can participate at larger financial levels than others. This can build a high level of resentment. When church members with limited resources are asked to pray about their commitments and respond, it should be celebrated even if their financial commitments are not among the major gifts. The story of the widow's response in Mark 12:41-44 validates this approach.

Some leaders make a mistake of concealing the costs of the campaign or the project, and this damages credibility. Eventually, there is an accounting of the finances of the campaign and project. When church members feel they have been misled, it is very difficult to re-build trust. The usual manifestation of this problem is when the church faces an unexpected debt load at the end of the three years of capital campaign contributions.

A lot of church members have been involved in capital campaigns for other institutions like a school, hospital, or library, and they think the church campaign should be similar. It is not unusual during a training meeting or a challenge for leadership gifts for the consultant or pastor to be admonished for being too "spiritual." This is a good teachable moment to make the distinction between a fundraiser and the nature and foundation of the church's capital campaign.

Sloppy methods and procedures also hurt a campaign. In one church, the communication director produced a brochure that missed the deadline for optimum effect, and because it was a last-minute project, the final brochure had photographs of all the steering committee that were so dark and poorly printed that no one could be recognized. This was not only poor production; it was embarrassing. It communicated that the brochure was not worth doing well and reduced the image of the campaign. Such sloppiness can be reduced by strong leadership from the steering committee.

External circumstances can also adversely affect a campaign. Zoning changes, cost overruns, neighborhood opposition, and labor or materials problems can delay a campaign and must be addressed openly. Delays in campaigns can enhance the subsequent effort when these problems are resolved.

One problem seen in a lot of campaigns is a change of leadership in the staff or the steering committee after the campaign has begun. Hopefully, any changes in staff can be projected and discussed during the pastor-preparation phase of the campaign. In churches with multiple staff, it is good to have staff orientation in addition to pastor preparation. Steering-committee members can be replaced, or in some cases their work can be completed by other steering-committee members. One leadership change that is more difficult to overcome is the departure of pastor or staff for negative reasons. Consideration then must be given to whether the campaign should be delayed.

Sometimes, expectations of a good relationship with professional counsel take a turn to dissatisfaction. Traits of the consultant that the church dislikes can include using too many stories, speaking too long at meetings, being insensitive to the church culture, or working too many campaigns at the same time and being road weary. Usually, if the consultant is made aware of the dissatisfaction, the problems can be resolved. Sometimes the consultant can be replaced from other available company consultants. As a last resort, if the contract has a buy-out clause, it can be exercised. Usually consultant problems are identified very early in the campaign and can be resolved quickly.

While this book has addressed the subject of campaign extensions or the need for multiple campaigns before, the two great concerns in this decision are usually whether a second or third campaign can achieve results as good as the first and whether a church can have campaign fatigue. In Illustration 5, church #38 is a first campaign and #42 is a second campaign in the same church three years later. In this illustration more was raised in the second campaign. The first campaign was for the purchase of land and the second campaign was for the first buildings on the land. In the second campaign, not only was there a broader base of support, but there were more and larger major gifts. The increase in the budget can also be seen. You should be aware, however, that a second campaign is not as well received when it is a surprise to the congregation.

Campaign fatigue is a reality in some settings. One young suburban church began their ministry with a commitment to having a three-year capital campaign every three years as far as they could see into the future. The church grew, and there was a fresh supply of new members for the campaigns for many years. After their fifth campaign, as they looked at their sixth, their growth had slowed and those people who had been in the church for fifteen years expressed that they needed a break. After waiting a couple of years and redeveloping their vision for the church, they entered another campaign and had the best results they had ever had. The difference was the delay and the focus that allowed increased ownership to develop.

An unusual but very real problem is the impact of an ill-defined or unrestricted endowment or the availability of undesignated reserves in a church on the results of a capital campaign. The quick answer is to define the purpose of the reserve or endowment funds. If church members are aware that the church has all the money it needs for the project, the motive for giving can be negated. The primary issue in this is the spiritual impact of not allowing people to grow spiritually in the process of a capital campaign to address church needs. A spectator attitude leads to detachment in more ways than just giving.

Most of the challenges in a capital campaign can be addressed by providing clear and open communication and having realistic expectations.

Chapter Eighteen

The Small-Church Campaign

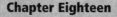

Challenges for the Small Church

The small-membership church faces some particular challenges when they need extraordinary funds for building, debt, or renovation. First, the small church is more likely to want to do the work through the labor and talents available within the church. This works well when it works well; but sometimes the donation of materials and services leads to control of the project by the few and lack of involvement of the many. On the other hand, when the work is to be contracted outside the church and funds are needed, the desire to raise the money in a short, circumvented process is even stronger. In the face of either of these challenges, financial results and the completion of a project can be achieved, but at what cost? One of the primary goals of the campaign is that the church members might develop a sense of spiritual purpose and understanding of God's will for their lives as they consider the church's direction. There is great value in a challenge to the entire church and the members' development of a new sense of unity and cooperation in a capital campaign.

Leadership can be a problem in the small-church capital campaign. In a small church, the influence of one or two families can be disproportionate in a bad or a good way. For instance, the project might be completed through underwriting by one or two patriarchal families who can also have primary influence on the design and scope of the project. This could discourage others from participating and create a sense of dependence upon those families. Churches often face serious problems when families on which they have been dependent move or die. Conversely, one or two families might make a challenging lead gift that would raise vision and encourage other members.

If the church has a need equal to its annual income or less, then the approach of using announcements and self-led effort may work. But if the need is for more than the church's annual income, a more structured capital campaign is needed. Small-church campaign programs are available from some denominational agencies. The costs are usually less and the program more basic in design. Some commercial firms have developed a small-church campaign program that is based on limited consultant leadership and the use of a standardized model with videotaped instruction. This is sometimes the best way a small church can have a successful campaign. We can define a small church as one with an annual income less than $75,000 or even $100,000 and with less than sixty families. A standardized program for a church of this size that can be implemented by the pastor and lay leadership is worth the cost.

Capital campaigns in smaller churches need to follow the same theological foundation and design as any other campaign. The difference is in the campaign design. Where larger churches need a larger steering committee with three or four levels of pyramidal enlistment, the smaller campaign can have a steering committee in which some of the positions are combined and only one level of enlistment is needed beyond the steering committee. The campaign can be shorter in length and use less communication materials because there are fewer people with whom to communicate. A simple fact sheet can be sent to every family, with home visitation taking the form of home or neighborhood gatherings. But the design should be specific and intentional. Designing and scheduling campaign activities can help overcome a casual approach that will result in indefinite commitments and a relaxed spiritual response. The key is still to inform the church members, to call them to prayer, to challenge those with greater financial ability to make large gifts, and to give a specific opportunity for everyone to respond.

The pastor's role is the same as it is in larger church campaigns but has some added challenges. The pastor of a small congregation is more likely to be either less experienced or in a retirement position. Certainly neither situation will increase the pastor's ability to design and direct a capital campaign. Like other pastors, he or she cannot do this alone. The role of the pastor discussed in earlier chapters is still applicable.

One very positive aspect of a small-church campaign is the increased fundraising capacity of the church that comes from the influence of one or two significant gifts. In terms of percentage, these gifts make a much more noticeable impact than the same amounts would in larger campaigns. In Illustration 5, churches one through five would represent small-church capital campaigns. For these churches, the average ratio of amount raised to annual budget is slightly higher than the overall ratio because of the influence of some $15,000 to $25,000 commitments. In church #11, which had a budget a little larger than most small churches have, the substantial amount raised was the direct result of three large gifts as well as a broad base of participation.

The small church not only can experience a financially successful capital campaign but can also experience the spiritual rewards. However, their effort needs to be intentional, planned, and based on a proven approach.

Chapter Nineteen

Naming Opportunities

Memorials and Tributes

Most churches have a culture and history with regard to naming opportunities. Churches have used a variety of ways to remember someone who has passed away with a memorial or honor someone who is highly respected. Some churches have a memorial tag on everything from windows to pews to chairs to hymnals. Other churches might have one or two buildings named for people based on a substantial financial gift or respect and fond memory. Other churches have policies against naming opportunities. This is a local-church issue. However, the issue does matter when a capital campaign is planned. Making a gift to name a building or a program is a regular practice in institutional capital campaigns. Most college buildings are named to honor people, and professorships and special courses of study are regularly used as memorial and tribute opportunities. There is inherent in the human heart a desire to remember the lives of those who have influenced worthwhile causes over the generations, as well as those whose commitments today set an inspiring example. Each church has to answer the question of whether memorial and tribute opportunities fit their church.

Helpful Approaches to Naming

If the church has no previously established precedent for memorial or tribute naming opportunities, the board or trustees should develop a policy prior to the capital campaign. This memorial and tribute policy should identify the terms of the opportunities, such as the item to be named, the amount of the commitment needed, and the method of recognition. For instance, when an organization decides to name a room or a building after a donor, it is usual for this donor to be an individual or a family—classes or other groups should not be considered for this type of donor recognition. These policies ought to be written and made available to everyone.

The items available for memorial and tribute recognition should be determined by the building committee with agreement from the board or trustees. The value of the item should be identified. The usual practice is for a naming opportunity to be secured by a commitment equal to anywhere from 51% to 100% of the cost of the item. The architect or contractor can assist in providing the costs of specific rooms or other items.

The method of recognition should be identified so that it might work within the church's standards of both aesthetics and appropriateness. Some churches use small brass memorial plaques and others want to use a memorial book. However, in the case of a particularly large gift such as a building or fellowship hall, something more substantial is appropriate.

Create a small brochure that presents the policy and the items and costs in an attractive way. The method of response by the donor and acceptance by the church of the gifts should be clearly explained. Resolving issues before they arise will help prevent difficult problems. For instance, stating that a gift must be complete before the naming occurs will help you avoid the awkward situation of having a name permanently attached to a building although the commitment was never completely fulfilled.

A Few Cautions

It is very important to get the facts correct. The amount of the gift, the nature of the recognition, and the spelling of the names all must be checked, rechecked, and confirmed again. Sometimes a donor will want to make a gift for something not planned in the capital campaign. For instance, one family wanted to make a substantial gift to name a chapel. There was not a chapel in the plans, so after a conversation, the family named the new church parlor in memory of a sister. It is also important not to offer a significant recognition for a modest gift. If a person with a $50,000 gift potential can name a classroom for giving only $10,000, the church might lose the value of the naming opportunity. It is also detrimental to have too many naming opportunities. When every chair, robe, window, pew, and door can be named, people with greater potential will sometimes make smaller gifts. Naming opportunities should only be at significant levels so the larger ones are not diminished by the smaller ones. For some reason, a lot of churches like to use some manner of buying bricks or using bricks for recognition. Such approaches very often lower expectation and seldom raise significant money. One church offered a brick for a gift of $1,000 or more. When it was pointed out that the courtyard where the bricks were going to be displayed would include more than ten thousand bricks, and only six hundred to eight hundred gifts of over $1,000 were expected, the church realized that the idea was less than dynamic. Not only would the "named" bricks be obscured by the nine thousand other bricks, but some families who could give more might limit their giving to $1000.

Memorials and tributes can be a meaningful expression in many churches and ought to be considered as a church plans a capital campaign. But the approach should be defined in advance and not emerge on the basis of suggestions by donors. Having policies that include items, values, and recognitions helps overcome the risk of donors changing the nature of projects.

In one historic downtown church during a self-led capital campaign, a $30,000 commitment led to the naming of a $500,000 chapel. In the context of the self-led effort, $30,000 was a large gift. The donor determined the value of the naming opportunity. However, in a subsequent, professionally led campaign, the least expensive naming opportunity was $50,000, and that caused hard feelings within the church family. Although there were some major gifts in the campaign, no gifts were received for memorials or tributes.

In a different historic downtown church, the capital campaign coincided with the retirement of a long-tenured, much-beloved pastor. The pastor was planning to retire the week after the announcement of the final results of the campaign. The reason for the timing was the feeling that to delay the campaign until the next pastor arrived would cause a delay of probably three years in the project. The new pastor would have to be appointed, settle in, and establish relationships before a campaign could be conducted. The project was one that had been discussed for several years and the timing seemed right. In respect for the pastor and his commitment and faithful service to the church, the new building was named in his honor. The church celebrated this substantial transition in church life in a lasting recognition.

Memorials and tributes can enhance a campaign in a church with a history of naming opportunities. But the process must be determined in advance of the campaign and be driven by a policy, not a donor.

Chapter Twenty

Where Do We Go From Here?

Concluding Comments

A lot of information has been considered in this book. One thing that has not been presented is how all of this information fits together into a coordinated program. The professional consultant will lay out the program for your church. Illustration 9 presents the phases and their activities in sequential order. The planning and organization/training phases represent as much as two thirds of the entire timeline for the campaign. The terminology used in Illustration 9 for the phases or the activities in the phases might be a little different depending on the consultant, but the content of the phases will be essentially the same.

This design can be used for purchasing new land, building new facilities, renovating existing facilities, and addressing debt and equipment needs. But in recent years this design has also been used to provide funding for missions, endowments, and special needs like denominational program support. Of course, many campaigns have several of these needs in combination. One church recently raised money for building, equipment, deferred maintenance of the building, the church endowment, a mission need, and a denominational campaign. But it is important to remember the spiritual value of the effort.

In order to complete the understanding of the church capital campaign, a contrast between the anticipated positive benefits and possible negative results needs to be explained. On the positive side, the church capital campaign can raise more than any other approach for funding; the costs of ministry are increasing dramatically, so safe-debt limits are diminishing rapidly. A capital campaign affords the church an excellent stewardship education opportunity. An intentional, professionally led campaign can help the church communicate its mission, ministry, and vision for the future. A well-designed and well-directed capital campaign can create a fresh enthusiasm for the church. During a campaign a church can identify, enlist, and train new leadership. Finally, a church capital campaign can enrich people's commitment to Christ and their church.

On the other hand, as beneficial as a church capital campaign can be for the individual spiritual journey as well as for the church body, there can also be some negative consequences. A capital campaign can become the church's entire ministry and a building can become its only vision. An effort entered without good financial planning can result in significant debt for completion of capital projects and substantial increases in needs for operational support. Sometimes a capital campaign can be predicated on the wrong presuppositions, like the value of a family life center in reclaiming younger members to an older downtown church. Sometimes alternatives to building are not seriously considered in the emotional appeal of a new building. Building programs can reflect cultural influences rather than spiritual purposes. A failed capital campaign can result in halting the church's momentum, including the possible loss of members. And a church capital campaign that isn't spiritually based can have an adverse effect on the church's ministry and mission revenue.

A capital campaign can represent a significant spiritual direction for the church. In 1 Chronicles 29:5 David issued a challenge: "Who then will offer willingly, consecrating themselves today to the LORD?" The challenge was a spiritual challenge expressed in financial terms. Later, in response in verse 9, we find the people rejoicing, giving willingly, and having a single mind. Ultimately, the response expected in a capital campaign has more to do with the heart than with the pocketbook. Jesus said that there is a relationship between our heart and our treasure. We take steps of faith when we respond to the challenge of offering willingly and consecrating ourselves to the Lord. Understanding the spiritual impact of a church capital campaign makes all the difference.

Illustrations

Illustration One

$300,000 Gift Profile Guide

This is an example of a typical gift profile guide. Each congregation will need to develop its own gift profile guide.

Number of Commitments	Amount of Each Commitment	Total Amount (No. of Commitments) X (Amount)	Cumulative Total
1	$36,000 ($1000 per month)	$36,000	$36,000
2	$18,000 ($500 per month)	$36,000	$72,000
3	$15,000 ($417 per month)	$45,000	$117,000
4	$10,000 ($278 per month)	$40,000	$157,000
8	$7,800 ($217 per month)	$62,400	$219,400
12	$3,600 ($100 per month)	$43,200	$262,600
Remainder	Less Than $3,600	$37,400	$300,000

Illustration Two

$500,000 Gift Profile Guide

This is an example of a typical gift profile guide. Each congregation will need to develop its own gift profile guide.

Number of Commitments	Amount of Each Commitment	Total Amount (No. of Commitments) X (Amount)	Cumulative Total
1	$75,000	$75,000	$75,000
2	$50,000	$100,000	$175,000
3	$25,000	$75,000	$250,000
4	$15,000	$60,000	$310,000
5	$10,000	$50,000	$360,000
8	$7,800	$62,400	$422,400
12	$3,600	$43,200	$465,600
Remainder	Less Than $3,600	$34,400	$500,000

Illustration Three

$1,000,000 Gift Profile Guide

This is an example of a typical gift profile guide. Each congregation will need to develop its own gift profile guide.

Number of Commitments	Amount of Each Commitment	Total Amount (No. of Commitments) X (Amount)	Cumulative Total
1	$150,000	$150,000	$150,000
3	$50,000	$150,000	$300,000
4	$36,000	$144,000	$444,000
6	$25,000	$150,000	$594,000
8	$15,000	$120,000	$714,000
10	$10,000	$100,000	$814,000
12	$5,000	$60,000	$874,000
20	$3,600	$72,000	$946,000
Remainder	Less Than $3,600	$54,000	$1,000,000

Illustration Four

$2,000,000 Gift Profile Guide

This is an example of a typical gift profile guide. Each congregation will need to develop its own gift profile guide.

Number of Commitments	Amount of Each Commitment	Total Amount (No. of Commitments) X (Amount)	Cumulative Total
1	$300,000	$300,000	$300,000
2	$150,000	$300,000	$600,000
2	$100,000	$200,000	$800,000
6	$50,000	$300,000	$1,100,000
6	$36,000	$216,000	$1,316,000
10	$25,000	$250,000	$1,566,000
10	$15,000	$150,000	$1,716,000
12	$10,000	$120,000	$1,836,000
15	$5,000	$75,000	$1,911,000
15	$3,600	$54,000	$1,965,000
Remainder	Less Than $3,600	$35,000	$2,000,000

Illustration Five

Results for Fifty Selected Capital Campaigns

Church Number	Income from Previous Year	Amount Raised in Capital Campaign	Ratio of Amount Raised to Previous Annual Income	Type of Project
1	$60,000	$111,500	1.86	Building
2	$62,000	$125,416	2.02	Building
3	$70,859	$178,960	2.53	Building
4	$100,800	$392,000	3.89	Building
5	$110,000	$373,000	3.39	Building
6	$124,132	$366,783	2.95	Building
7	$125,000	$251,000	2.01	Building
8	$133,236	$485,690	3.65	Building
9	$140,000	$336,500	2.40	Building
10	$140,000	$418,000	2.99	Building
11	$143,000	$630,564	4.41	Relocation
12	$153,000	$465,000	3.04	Buy Land
13	$168,000	$515,000	3.07	Building
14	$174,623	$494,926	2.83	Building
15	$182,205	$329,631	1.81	Building
16	$191,000	$220,000	1.15	Buy Land
17	$198,000	$396,000	2.00	Building
18	$200,966	$688,320	3.43	Building
19	$208,000	$383,336	1.84	Building
20	$209,000	$830,000	3.97	Building
21	$230,000	$525,000	2.28	Building
22	$233,341	$770,000	3.30	Building
23	$237,000	$372,047	1.57	Debt/ Renovation
24	$248,348	$931,427	3.75	Building
25	$255,000	$605,643	2.38	Building
26	$278,000	$496,000	1.78	Renovation
27	$283,780	$683,164	2.41	Building

Church Number	Income from Previous Year	Amount Raised in Capital Campaign	Ratio of Amount Raised to Previous Annual Income	Type of Project
28	$303,000	$479,000	1.58	Renovation
29	$310,141	$851,000	2.74	Building
30	$345,536	$663,324	1.92	Building
31	$350,000	$926,161	2.65	Building
32	$390,000	$1,223,136	3.14	Renovation
33	$392,000	$515,000	1.31	Debt/Renovation
34	$395,059	$872,942	2.21	Renovation/Building
35	$421,000	$880,000	2.09	Building
36	$438,680	$744,000	1.70	Renovation
37	$440,000	$512,000	1.16	Renovation
38	$463,000	$1,552,613	3.35	Buy Land
39	$470,606	$923,470	1.96	Renovation
40	$471,859	$1,037,000	2.20	Renovation
41	$503,438	$1,029,000	2.04	Renovation/Building
42	$550,000	$2,541,986	4.62	Relocation
43	$589,690	$2,524,767	4.28	Building
44	$633,049	$1,307,331	2.07	Debt/Building
45	$686,500	$944,788	1.38	Debt/Renovation/Building
46	$695,000	$982,000	1.41	Debt
47	$713,129	$1,825,588	2.56	Building
48	$754,493	$1,850,000	2.45	Building
49	$777,255	$2,022,325	2.60	Building
50	$802,794	$1,466,000	1.83	Debt
50 Campaigns		$40,048,338	2.52	

Illustration Six

Cash-Flow Analysis—Summary

Historical Data

Annual Income	$250,000
Existing Loan Amount	$ 0
Existing Annual Loan Payment	$ 0

Building Campaign

Projected Construction Costs		$500,000
Contingency (architect, engineer, change orders, etc.)	15%	$ 75,000
TOTAL PROJECT COSTS		**$575,000**

Pledges collected over	3 years	$500,000
Collection begins	4/01	
Collection ends	3/04	
Average collection	85%	**$425,000**
Cash on hand for project		$ 0

Assumptions

Income grows 5% as a result of expansion.
The amount that can be set aside for debt is 33.3%

The following growth is projected to occur:

	Year One	Year Two	Year Three
Operating Income	$262,500	$275,625	$289,406
Loan Payment Budget	$4,163	$8,533	$13,122

Results

At an interest rate of 8.00%,
yearly payments of $13,122 over 15 years
will support a loan of **$114,424**

As shown on the loan amortization (Illustration 7), after completing the capital campaign the church would have a loan balance of **$205,355**.

Illustration Seven
Cash-Flow Analysis—Loan Amortization

Date	Pledge Collection	Interest Payment (8%)	Principal Payments	Cash Balance	Loan Balance
4/01	11,805.56			11,805.56	
5/01	11,805.56			23,611.11	
6/01	11,805.56			35,416.67	
7/01	11,805.56			47,222.22	
8/01	11,805.56			59,027.78	
9/01	11,805.56			70,833.33	
10/01	11,805.56			82,638.89	
11/01	11,805.56		(95,833.33)		1,388.89
12/01	11,805.56	9.26	(95,833.33)		85,425.93
1/02	11,805.56	569.51	(95,833.33)		170,023.21
2/02	11,805.56	1,133.49	(95,833.33)		255,184.48
3/02	11,805.56	1,701.23	(95,833.33)		340,913.48
4/02	11,805.56	2,272.76	(95,833.33)		427,214.02
Permanent Loan Amortization Begins					
5/02	11,805.56	2,848.09	8,957.46		418,256.56
6/02	11,805.56	2,788.38	9,017.18		409,239.38
7/02	11,805.56	2,728.26	9,077.29		400,162.08
8/02	11,805.56	2,667.75	9,137.81		391,024.28
9/02	11,805.56	2,606.83	9,198.73		381,825.55
10/02	11,805.56	2,545.50	9,260.05		372,565.50
11/02	11,805.56	2,483.77	9,321.79		363,243.71
12/02	11,805.56	2,421.62	9,383.93		353,859.78
1/03	11,805.56	2,359.07	9,446.49		344,413.29
2/03	11,805.56	2,296.09	9,509.47		334,903.82
3/03	11,805.56	2,232.69	9,572.86		325,330.96
4/03	11,805.56	2,168.87	9,636.68		315,694.28
5/03	11,805.56	2,104.63	9,700.93		305,993.35
6/03	11,805.56	2,039.96	9,765.60		296,227.75
7/03	11,805.56	1,974.85	9,830.70		286,397.05
8/03	11,805.56	1,909.31	9,896.24		276,500.80
9/03	11,805.56	1,843.34	9,962.22		266,538.59
10/03	11,805.56	1,776.92	10,028.63		256,509.96
11/03	11,805.56	1,710.07	10,095.49		246,414.47
12/03	11,805.56	1,642.76	10,162.79		236,251.67
1/04	11,805.56	1,575.01	10,230.54		226,021.13
2/04	11,805.56	1,506.81	10,298.75		215,722.38
3/04	11,805.56	1,438.15	10,367.41		205,354.98
	$425,000.16	$55,354.98	$221,859.04		$205,354.98

Illustration Eight

Approximate Commercial Fees for Capital Campaigns

This chart gives an approximate range of the fees that a church can expect to pay for the use of a professional campaign consultant. These are provided for general information only. Each consulting firm establishes its own fee schedule.

Church Annual Budget	Approximate Commercial Fees
Less than $60,000	$5,000 – $10,000
$60,000 – $100,000	$10,000 – $15,000
$100,000 – $150,000	$15,000 – $22,000
$150,000 – $200,000	$20,000 – $26,000
$200,000 – $300,000	$24,000 – $32,000
$300,000 – $400,000	$28,000 – $38,000
$400,000 – $500,000	$32,000 – $45,000
$500,000 – $600,000	$35,000 – $45,000
$600,000 – $700,000	$38,000 – $48,000
$700,000 – $800,000	$42,000 – $54,000
$800,000 – $1,000,000	$48,000 – $60,000
$1,000,000 – $1,500,000	$62,000 – $85,000
$1,500,000 – $2,000,000	$65,000 – $90,000
$2,000,000 – $2,500,000	$75,000 – $120,000
$2,500,000 – $3,000,000	$100,000 – $125,000
$3,000,000 – $4,000,000	$120,000 – $140,000
$4,000,000 – $5,000,000	$130,000 – $180,000
$5,000,000 – up	$150,000 – up

Illustration Nine

Campaign Phases

This chart shows the general flow of a capital campaign. While this is illustrated in a linear format there will be a time overlap between the phases. Individual consulting firms may use different names for each of these stages, but most capital campaign programs will follow a process very similar to the one illustrated here.

Planning	Organization and Training	Project Awareness and Prayer Support
Program is planned Calendar is coordinated Steering committee is selected Manual is prepared Program is introduced to the congregation	The following teams are enlisted and trained: • Home-Visitation • Communications • Hospitality • Leader-Commit-ment • Congregational commitment	Home visits occur Information gatherings are held Information is distributed Audiovisuals are shown and displayed Prayer support is organized and encouraged

Education, Information, and Inspiration	Major Event	Commitment	Encourage-ment and Reporting
Sermons related to the campaign emphasis are preached Statements of support are presented Bible studies are held Communication is provided through news-letters, posters, an information booth, and so forth. Leaders are asked to make a commitment Hospitality calls are made	Congregation-wide celebration takes place, focusing on the vision for ministry and growth Advance-commitment total from leaders is announced Congregation is encouraged and prepared for receiving commitments as scheduled	Commitments are received as agreed between campaign leaders and consultant	Follow-up activities are planned to encourage immediate giving, faithful giving, and new giving